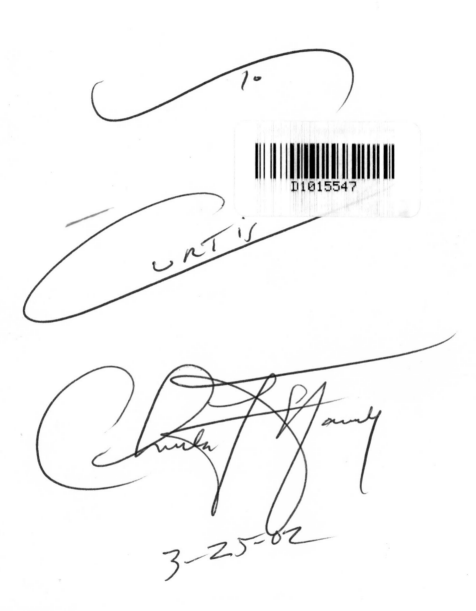

To

Curtis

D1015547

3-25-02

WALKING
WISELY

REAL GUIDANCE FOR LIFE'S JOURNEY

CHARLES F. STANLEY

THOMAS NELSON PUBLISHERS®
Nashville

A Division of Thomas Nelson, Inc.
www.ThomasNelson.com

Published by Thomas Nelson Publishers, a Division of Thomas Nelson, Inc.,
P.O. Box 141000, Nashville, Tennessee, 37214.

Library of Congress Cataloging-in-Publication Data

Stanley, Charles F.
    Walking wisely : real guidance for life's journey / Charles Stanley.
        p. cm.
    ISBN 0-7852-7298-4 (hc)
    1. Christian life—Baptist authors. 2. Wisdom—Religious aspects—Christianity.
I. Title.

BV4509.5 .S82 2002
241'.4—dc21   2001054681

Printed in the United States of America
02 03 04 05 06 BVG 9 8 7 6 5 4 3 2 1

This book is dedicated to Steve Yungerberg,
a faithful, loyal, and devoted friend who has encouraged me
and helped me to walk wisely through the seasons
of both adversity and joy.

Wisdom is the principal thing;
Therefore get wisdom.

—PROVERBS 4:7

CONTENTS

ONLY TWO WAYS TO WALK

There are only two ways to walk in this life—wisely or unwisely. There are only two types of choices—wise or unwise.

Throughout the Scriptures God admonishes His people to walk wisely. His Word declares boldly:

> Happy is the man who finds wisdom,
> And the man who gains understanding;
> For her proceeds are better than the profits of silver,
> And her gain than fine gold.
> She is more precious than rubies,
> And all the things you may desire cannot compare with her.
> Length of days is in her right hand,
> In her left hand riches and honor.
> Her ways are ways of pleasantness,
> And all her paths are peace.

She is a tree of life to those who take hold of her,
And happy are all who retain her. (Prov. 3:13–18)

Nothing man may acquire, earn, or achieve in the natural realm is as valuable as wisdom. One of the reasons God places such a high value on wisdom is no doubt because the stakes related to living wisely are so high. If you choose to walk wisely, here's what you can expect:

- *Contentment*—beyond happiness into the realm of pure joy, based upon an abiding knowledge within your spirit that your life has a purpose

- *Courage*—from having faith that God is with you at all times, in all situations, and that He *will* defeat the enemy of your soul and bring you to wholeness

- *Confidence*—born of knowing that God loves you with an everlasting, unconditional love

- *Peace*—rooted in the knowledge that God is working all things for your eternal benefit

- *Progress*—based upon your belief that forgiveness, mercy, renewal, and growth are God's plan for every believer

- *Prosperity*—to the degree that God chooses to pour His spiritual, emotional, and material blessings into your life

The person who walks in wisdom experiences God's presence, power, and wonderful, boundless approval.

On the other hand, if you choose to walk unwisely, you can expect a far different set of outcomes:

- *Conflict*—not only with others, but in your own mind and soul

- *Consternation*—anxiety, worry, and fear of the future, including a fear of entering eternity

- *Disappointment*—the "unsettled" feeling that there must be more to life than what you are experiencing

- *Disillusionment*—a persistent degree of deep, inner bitterness and resentment that life hasn't turned out the way you had hoped, expected, or desired

- *Discontentment*—that gnaws continually at your soul, leading you to seek satisfaction in the fleshly lusts of human nature

If a person chooses habitually to walk apart from wisdom, he can expect God's disapproval of his life. If he walks without wisdom long enough and excludes God from his life until the day he dies, he will die without Christ as his Savior and spend eternity separated from God.

The truth of God's Word is very clear: You never lose if you choose to live wisely. You always lose if you choose to live foolishly.

If the consequences are so clear-cut, why is it that the majority of people, including many Christians, choose *not* to pursue wisdom with their whole heart?

Walking in wisdom is difficult. I make no claim that it is easy to walk wisely, or that it is without obstacles. To walk wisely day in and day out is one of the most challenging things any person can ever face.

Most Christians know that when they go through a difficult

time, they are wise to keep their eyes on the Lord. It is difficult, however, not to become afraid and to falter in our faith.

Most Christians know that when they are faced with temptation, the wise response is to say "no." It is difficult to do so, however, if a loved one presents the temptation or there is social pressure to participate.

Most Christians know that it is wise to forgive a person who has wronged them. Still, it is difficult to do, especially if immense emotional, physical, or material harm has taken place.

Most Christians know that it is wise to tithe their income. It is difficult to do, especially when a person has debt or has serious financial pressures.

Most Christians know that it is wise to witness about Jesus Christ. It is difficult to do, however, when it places our reputation or career on the line due to office politics.

How can we walk in wisdom when there are so many voices clamoring for us to ignore God's wisdom and pursue our own desires? This book aims to answer these and many other questions. The good news is that God's Word has the answers—not only to these questions but also to *any* question a person may ask. God's Word provides answers related to our beliefs, our relationships, and our behavior in very practical areas of life. The Bible is a comprehensive manual for *how* to walk in wisdom.

As you read this book, I encourage you to pray these words continually: "Father, please give me Your wisdom." I have no doubt if you pray with a humble and sincere heart, God will give you His wisdom. His delight is to impart to you what will ultimately give you joy, peace, and blessings.

ONE

The Challenge of God's Word: Walk in Wisdom

During a break in a Christmas pageant rehearsal, a young boy came running up to the pastor and announced, "I'm a wise man!"

"You are?" said the pastor. "You seem pretty excited about it."

The boy beamed. "I am!"

"What's so great about being a wise man?" the pastor asked.

The boy quickly replied, "I get to carry the gold . . . and I don't have to hang around any smelly ol' sheep."

Many people in our world today seem to have a similar view of wisdom. They believe wisdom is the ability to "carry the gold"—to make a good living, to live a comfortable life, and to avoid association with anything unpleasant.

I believe God's Word points us to a different definition of wisdom:

Wisdom is the capacity to see things from God's perspective
and to respond to them according to scriptural principles.

In other words wisdom is seeking heavenly opinions on earthly circumstances.

There are five main reasons God desires for us to walk in wisdom:

1. God desires for us to become all that He created us to be. He expects us to develop and then to use all of the talents, abilities, and gifts that He has placed within us. He desires for us to maximize our potential—to become the man or woman He created us to be.

2. God desires for us to accomplish all of the work that He sets before us to do. God does not call us to unfinished tasks or halfhearted ventures. When God places a challenge, opportunity, or goal in front of us, He expects us to pursue it with the whole heart, mind, and soul *and* to experience a measure of success in *accomplishing* what He has called us to do.

3. God desires for us to receive, to experience, and to enjoy all the blessings He desires to pour into our lives. God wants us to walk wisely so that we may experience the fullness of His provision as promised in His Word. He *wants* us to have the fruit born of wise choices and decisions. He *wants* us to be spiritually prosperous, to be physically and emotionally healthy, and to have our financial and material needs met.

4. God desires for our lives to bring glory to Him. God wants us to live in a way that causes others to want Christ Jesus in their lives. The foolish life does not bring glory to God; the wise life does.

5. God desires that we avoid all the pitfalls associated with

foolish living. We may not be able to quickly answer the question, "How do we walk wisely?" but most of us have a pretty good idea as to why people act foolishly.

First, some foolish choices are made in ignorance. We act in error—not really knowing what we don't know, and at times, not taking time to find out what we *should* know before embarking on a course of action or entering a relationship.

Sometimes our ignorance is rooted in bad counsel. We seek out the wrong people for advice or direction. We get bad information about what to do, to think, to say, to believe, or to choose.

Sometimes we never even think to ask the question, "Am I being wise?" The concept of wisdom never lodges in our minds. We are totally oblivious to the fact that we can experience wisdom or should seek it.

Second, foolish choices are often rooted in self-gratification. The law of self-gratification says: I want what I want . . . when I want it . . . how I want it . . . as often as I want it . . . to the degree I want it.

Third, some foolish choices are made in response to peer or societal pressure. The world does not value wisdom, and most people choose to go with the flow of society as a whole. Many people assume that because "everybody is doing it," a certain behavior or choice must be acceptable, at least to some degree. They never even stop to question whether a behavior is wise or foolish—they simply react to life as others around them are reacting.

As a whole, we human beings want to be entertained and satisfied far more than we want to be challenged. We want to take the easy path of least resistance because to do otherwise involves effort, change, and discipline.

The Ultimate Fool's Game

The fool's game is believing that "I can live my life *my way* and win." Such a life is marked by rebellion, disobedience, and pride. God simply will *not* bless or reward such a life.

You can tell me all about your degrees, experience, background, credentials, accomplishments, notoriety, fame, fortune, and awards, but if you are rejecting God in your life, you are still playing the fool's game. The most important thing you can do in your life is to receive Jesus Christ as your personal Savior.

An Inevitable Appointment

Only foolish people avoid, deny, ignore, and delay decisions that are inevitable. One such decision involves eternity. You *will* die. The Bible says, "It is appointed for men to die once, but after this the judgment" (Heb. 9:27).

You may not believe there is a judgment after death, but you certainly must believe that you will face death. You only need to look around with a little objectivity to realize that you have never met a two-hundred-year-old person. Death is not a might, maybe, or perhaps event—it is an inevitable event of every person's life. Even if a person experiences the second coming of Christ, he will undergo a change or a transformation that will be as definitive as death. A *wise* person faces the inevitabilities of life, especially the inevitability of death.

AN INEVITABLE JUDGMENT

What about the inevitability of God's judgment? Consider this: When you look at the whole of God's creation, has *anything* been created without a plan and purpose? The natural world provides thousands—yes, millions and perhaps billions—of examples of cause and effect, action and response, and behavior and consequence. It is only rational to conclude that God—who created everything in this universe and established all of the natural laws to govern His universe—would include a purpose for man's life that includes cause and effect, action and response, and behavior and consequence. Who we become in this life and what we do in this life are subject to divine evaluation—not only daily, but also eternally.

A judgment awaits each one of us after we die. Only a foolish person would ignore that fact or fail to prepare for a divine evaluation of his or her life.

DAILY REJECTION OF GOD'S PLAN

By rejecting God, of course, I am not talking only about God's offer of salvation and eternal life through Jesus Christ. Many believers reject God in their daily lives by ignoring the commandments of God, the moral parameters established by God, and the wise counsel of God's Word. They overlook the promptings, urgings, and intuitive impulses of the Holy Spirit. They remain intent on living life according to their own strength and ability. They rely on their own résumés, resources, and intellect to see them through difficult times. And in rejecting God in these often subtle, routine, and socially acceptable ways, they, too, are playing the fool's game.

Any time a person limits the role of God in his life or compromises God's commandments, that person is rejecting Him.

The sad news is that we suffer consequences of foolishness even if we don't *know* we are being foolish or are rejecting God. In fact, the vast majority of people don't recognize that they are walking foolishly until they experience the consequences of their unwise choices and behaviors.

THE QUESTION THAT FOLLOWS ERROR: "WHAT HAPPENED?"

People often find themselves dazed or stunned by the consequences of their lives. They seem genuinely surprised that they are experiencing negative consequences as the result of unwise choices and decisions. They ask, "What happened? What did I do to deserve this?"

People usually don't think about their health until they are sick. They don't think about the state of their finances until they are facing retirement without sufficient funds or foreclosure and bankruptcy because their spending has surpassed their income.

They don't think about the way they parent until one of their children goes astray or makes a bad choice. They don't think about their relationships with others until they find themselves in an unending argument or an impasse of some kind.

What happened? Each person is responsible for making his or her own decisions and choices, true—but was God involved? Did each person ask God to reveal His wisdom on a matter before he or she acted or spoke? No. The person did not take positive precautionary or preventive measures. In still other cases, the person chose to associate with people who were an influence for evil, not for good.

Foolish choices tend to result in a "snowballing" of further foolish choices. One bad decision leads to another bad decision, and the result is very costly.

GOD DESIRES A BETTER WAY

The apostle Paul wrote this challenge from God to the Ephesians:

> See then that you walk circumspectly, not as fools but as wise, redeeming the time, because the days are evil. Therefore do not be unwise, but understand what the will of the Lord is. (Eph. 5:15–17)

In these two verses, God makes three things very clear:

1. We must choose to pursue wisdom. It's up to each of us to determine *how* we will walk through this life. Wisdom is not something a person stumbles into or acquires automatically; it must be sought out and pursued.

2. We must seek God's plan. The person who walks in wisdom

is very aware of his life, how he affects the world, and how the world affects him. He recognizes that every person faces three enemies in life: the world system, the flesh, and the devil. He seeks to know God's plan and purpose—not only for his personal life but also for every situation involving other people around him.

God's promise is that those who love and search for wisdom *will* find it. "Wisdom" speaks in Proverbs 8:17, saying, "I love those who love me, and those who seek me diligently will find me." Jesus echoed this when He said, "Ask, and it will be given to you; seek, and you will find; knock, and it will be opened to you. For everyone who asks receives, and he who seeks finds, and to him who knocks it will be opened" (Matt. 7:7–8).

3. We must take responsibility for applying wisdom to our lives. The person who walks in wisdom feels a responsibility for her own actions and use of time. She knows that she has been given a limited quantity of minutes, hours, days, months, and years. She knows that she must spend those hours in a way that produces the largest amount of good. She also knows that God has entrusted her with certain material resources that must be used to maximally further God's purposes on the earth.

We are called to be wise in every decision of our lives. We need God's wisdom in our business dealings, our health, our relationships, our parenting, our finances, and our relationship with Him. No area of life is beyond the need for wisdom, off-limits to God's wisdom, or ignored by God's Word. God's wisdom can be readily applied to every decision or choice we make, every relationship we have, every emotion we feel, every action we take, every opinion we hold, and every idea or challenge we pursue.

Furthermore, the person who walks wisely is acutely aware of the enemy of his soul who seeks to enslave him, the temptations that seek to ensnare him, and the world's systems that seek to entrap him. He lives his life with soberness and caution, saying "no" to *anything* that undermines the potential for receiving God's highest blessings.

Wisdom is something we choose to live out. It is not a vague entity. Wisdom is related to the concrete, material, tangible, real world. It is a *way* of approaching every relationship, every decision, every choice, every problem or opportunity, and every circumstance of life.

The title of this book is *Walking Wisely.* I want to emphasize the word *walking.* We walk two congruent and simultaneous paths in life: We walk *with* God, and we walk *with* other people. We need wisdom primarily about *how* to walk wisely in our relationship with God and to grow in our relationship with Him. We need God's wisdom about *how* to build relationships that are deep, lasting, purposeful, and godly. Although we certainly need God's best strategies for dealing with other practical areas of life, these two areas of wisdom are paramount to every person, every day. These areas will be our focus. If we walk in wisdom with God and other people, we are likely to know, to apply, and to live in God's wisdom in all other circumstances as well.

WISDOM IS AVAILABLE TO EVERY PERSON

The good news about God's wisdom is this: Every person *can* become wise. That isn't true for fame, fortune, or education. Not all people have the intellectual ability to earn college degrees. Not all people have the talents or attributes that contribute to fame. Not all people have the skills and opportunities necessary for acquiring wealth.

But every person can reverence God, can receive Jesus Christ as Savior, and can submit his or her life to God on a daily basis. *Every* person can become wise.

Will *you* accept God's challenge to become a wise person and to walk in His wisdom daily?

TWO

EARTHLY WISDOM VERSUS GODLY WISDOM

If someone were to ask you today, "Are you a wise person?" how would you respond?

Many people would respond, "Well, I'd like to be."

Some people seem to think that wise people are locked away in ivory towers—they perceive wisdom to be a function of intellect or brain power applied to areas such as philosophy, theology, or psychology. Others believe a wise person must be aged. Still others think it is a good thing to be wise—but a pretentious thing to admit. They secretly believe they are wise but are reluctant to say so because they fear others will think ill of them.

If you consider yourself to be a wise person, what is your basis for reaching that conclusion?

TWO VERY DIFFERENT VIEWS OF WISDOM

The world and God's Word present two very different views of wisdom. From God's perspective, earthly wisdom—human

15

or natural wisdom—is grounded in man's fallen nature. Godly wisdom—divine or spiritual wisdom—is based upon man's "new nature" given at the time of a person's spiritual rebirth (2 Cor. 5:17).

All godly wisdom begins with reverence—an understanding of who our sovereign, almighty God is, and out of that understanding, surrendering one's will and behavior to Him. There is no alternative foundation on which genuine wisdom can be built.

A person may say, "Do you mean to tell me that with all of my education and experience, I cannot be wise if I don't receive God's forgiveness for my sin and factor God into my life?" That's exactly what I mean to tell you! And I say this not out of my own human understanding—that's what the Word of God says. Apart from God, a human being *cannot* function in wisdom.

THE FOUNDATION FOR WALKING WISELY

Proverbs 9:10 tells us, "The fear of the LORD is the beginning of wisdom." "Fear" in this verse refers to reverence for God. Those who fear God stand in awe of God. They have at least a glimmer of understanding that God is omniscient (all-wise), omnipotent (all-powerful), omnipresent (present in every moment and throughout all eternity), and all-loving, and that they are not. They stand before God in wonderment and amazement that God, who is all, has all, and controls all, cares, loves, reaches out, and blesses the individual human being. To fear God is not to fear God's judgment; it is to stand in awe that God has all authority to judge and to forgive, to show mercy, and to grant His grace in overflowing abundance.

Spiritual wisdom is given to those who accept Jesus Christ as their Savior, commit themselves to following God in obedience, seek to develop a relationship with Him, reverence Him, and walk out their days submitted to, yielded to, and listening to the Holy Spirit.

Let me ask you . . .

Are you wiser than God your Creator is when it comes to knowing how to live a successful life on this earth?

Are you wiser than God, who made your body, when it comes to knowing how to live in health?

Are you wiser than God, who caused you to be born in a specific time and place, to a specific set of parents, in a specific set of circumstances, when it comes to developing a plan and purpose for your life?

Are you wiser than God, who created all natural resources and everything of real value on this earth, when it comes to knowing how to manage your finances and material resources?

Are you wiser than God, who made human nature, when it comes to knowing how to develop and maintain good relationships?

Who would be so foolish as to say he or she is wiser than the Creator and sovereign King of this universe? How ridiculously arrogant to say in the face of God, "I know more than You do. I know better than You know. I have a better idea than Your idea."

GETTING GOD'S UNLIMITED VIEW OF OUR LIVES

Wisdom is the capacity to see things from God's viewpoint. A child once was asked if he knew the meaning of the word *omniscient*. He said, "Yes. My mom taught me that word. It means that God knows everything about everything." I can't beat that definition.

God knows what we feel, what we think, who we are, and how we function. He knows our likes, dislikes, dreams, desires, fears, and hurts. He knows what brings us joy, peace, and feelings of fulfillment. As our "Maker" He knows every detail of our "makeup"!

God also knows every detail about every circumstance we encounter. He sees the beginning from the ending, and every step between the beginning and the ending.

Earthly wisdom is limited. It generally is based upon the best that collective humanity has been able to conclude or to decipher. Earthly wisdom says, "This is the way men and women have acted, responded, and lived through the ages." Earthly wisdom concludes, "This is what works." Earthly wisdom can be very narrow, and it is usually filled with biases, prejudices, and personal desires.

God's wisdom, in contrast, is unlimited. It is based upon what God sees when He looks to ages past and ahead to ages still to come. It is based upon the whole of any given life or situation. Godly wisdom says, "This is the way I made man to act, respond, and succeed." Godly wisdom concludes, "This is what God wants."

If we want to be wise, we must choose to see things from God's perspective. We must get God's "take" on a situation. Not only must we ask, "How does God see this?" but also, "What does God want me to do? When? How? With whom? For what goal or purpose?" We must seek to see our individual lives as fitting into God's plan, God's purpose, and God's desires. The Bible makes this very clear:

> He who trusts in his own heart is a fool,
> But whoever walks wisely will be delivered. (Prov. 28:26)

FOUR MAIN ERRORS OF EARTHLY WISDOM

Earthly wisdom is based on these four faulty conclusions:

1. Wisdom is limited to the mind of man.
2. Wisdom is based on what can be perceived by the five human senses.
3. Wisdom is doing what man collectively defines as rational or provable.
4. Wisdom is doing "whatever works."

God's truth about wisdom is one hundred and eighty degrees opposite each of these humanly constructed conclusions.

GOD'S WISDOM: MAN'S KNOWLEDGE IS NOT ENOUGH

We live in the so-called information age. We have more information today than we know how to process and use. Those of us who have home computers have more information than we will ever access just several clicks away. Even when we are trying to relax, we have information foisted on us—pagers beep, phones ring, televisions blare, and computers announce that a new electronic message is waiting for our response.

For all of our information, have we increased in wisdom? No. We only need to take a look at recent political history to gain an understanding that knowledge and wisdom are different. Many highly knowledgeable people work for our government. Each makes it his life's work to become informed about certain issues, as well as about history, economics, and the law. But do they always live wisely? Do they always pass laws that are in line with God's Word? Do they always live moral lives that are yielded to God's will?

Take a look at our educational system. It has been developed through the years by people who have been considered to be highly knowledgeable when it comes to child psychology, child development, curriculum formation, instructional methods, and information resources. But are our children being trained in wisdom? Is God factored into their learning process? Is godly behavior being emphasized? Is faith being encouraged? Generally speaking, no.

Intellectually gifted people are not necessarily wise. Neither are those who have developed their natural skills and abilities to the maximum of their potential, those who have established the "best contacts" in the world, those who have amassed fabulous wealth, or those who have spent their lives in pursuit of the best health possible. Never assume that in becoming informed or knowledgeable, you will become wise.

Furthermore, at no place in the Scriptures do we see God rewarding an increase in knowledge. Repeatedly, however, we find God calling His people to an increase in wisdom and promising to reward those who walk according to godly principles.

The Proper Place for Knowledge and Understanding. Knowledge is something acquired by mental study and observation. Knowledge is important—I am not at all denigrating the value of knowledge. All knowledge is a gift of God. God allows us to know, to discover, and to grow in knowledge. Certainly knowledge of the Scriptures acquired by study is vital to a person's spiritual growth. So is a knowledge of godly behavior gained by observing the lives of strong Christians.

Knowledge, however, is limited. No person can know all there is to know about any subject, person, or situation. There is always something unknown or as yet undiscovered.

It takes the Holy Spirit of God to pull back the curtains of our understanding. The Holy Spirit reveals to us insights as to why certain things happen and how certain situations might be resolved. The Holy Spirit imparts to us deeper insights into His commandments and precepts and the blessings that come in following them.

The Bible declares, "Get wisdom! Get understanding!" (Prov. 4:5). The two are not the same. Understanding is based upon the acquisition of knowledge—it is a filtering, sifting, sorting, and defining process. Wisdom, in comparison, is an applying process.

Understanding tells us what is happening—wisdom tells us why it is happening. Understanding gives us the facts—wisdom tells us what to do with those facts. Understanding yields insight into how a problem might be solved—wisdom tells us which solution to pursue, and when and how to pursue it.

Does a wise person know everything? No. However, I believe strongly that only a wise person is capable of using knowledge to maximum advantage. A wise person is capable of determining which facts, concepts, principles, or procedures to use in a given situation. A wise person knows the criteria of God's Word for successful financial investments, successful health management, and successful relationships. A wise person knows how to apply what he learns.

In my life, I have met a number of wise people who had very little formal education. Even so, they had a keen ability to discern, to perceive, and to understand God's principles . . . and their wise choices and decisions have led each to become a powerful, influential, successful, and in some cases, wealthy individual.

I have met a number of godly men and women who never went to seminary, never learned Greek or Hebrew, and never studied theology. Nevertheless, they live according to God's wisdom and are accomplishing much for God on this earth. They are preaching Bible-based sermons, engaging in innovative missionary work, teaching their children to love the Lord, and winning their neighbors to Christ. Their reward will be great, even though they have never earned a degree in religion or gained a reputation for ministry distinction in the eyes of man.

On the other hand, I have also met a number of highly educated, highly accomplished, highly talented, very well-informed people who have made foolish decisions and choices in their lives, and the end result has been catastrophic for them and their families.

GOD'S WISDOM: DISCERNMENT BEYOND THE FIVE SENSES

The world says that wisdom is based upon what a person can perceive with his natural senses. God's wisdom calls for a person to walk in the discerning power of the Holy Spirit, who is not at all limited by human senses.

The Holy Spirit enables a person to discern what isn't spoken and what isn't readily manifested. The Holy Spirit gives a "heart sense" to a person so that the person has an ability to recognize truth from lie, fact from fiction, right from wrong—regardless of the words that may be spoken or the alluring images that may be presented.

The person who walks in godly wisdom has a "sense" or intuition provided by the Holy Spirit, who lives inside of every believer. I strongly believe that the person who functions in godly wisdom is able to see beyond what average human beings see . . . able to hear beyond what average human beings hear . . . able to understand beyond what average human beings understand. This ability flows directly from the Holy Spirit at work in us.

I can't begin to count the number of times I have heard godly men and women tell me, "I started to take one action and then I had this little feeling deep inside me that I should wait . . . or take a different action . . . or get additional information." That "little feeling" for the believer is the Holy Spirit at work, guarding us, guiding us, and moving us into the center of God's path for us to walk.

Earthly wisdom based upon the five human senses can often produce confusion. What one sees, another doesn't. What one hears, another doesn't.

Earthly wisdom often leads to a skewed perspective, especially if it is based upon collective perception. Large masses of people can become convinced that they see, feel, hear, or otherwise perceive a lie.

The result of faulty human perception frequently leads to the establishment of goals that are off target and unproductive in the things that truly matter for eternity.

In sharp contrast, the wisdom given by the Holy Spirit yields clarity and precision. It leads to an expansion of ability, a righteous perspective, and the establishment of goals that are focused and productive, and that are centered on the most important things of eternal benefit.

The presence of the Holy Spirit expands a person's ability to perceive so that a person "sees" life in the context of eternity. The person who walks in godly wisdom does not make decisions on the basis of how things look on the surface at any given time. What he perceives is placed against the template of heaven's understanding and will.

Discernment Is Especially Important in Crisis Times. Even ungodly people will admit that in times of crisis or natural catastrophe, people don't think clearly. Our perception becomes clouded when we are under intense emotional pressure or time constraints. It is in times of crisis that we especially need the discerning power of the Holy Spirit at work in our lives.

Certainly none of us succeed at everything all the time. All of us face crises and calamities. But God's wisdom does help us walk through times of difficulty, hardship, suffering, and persecution and emerge stronger.

The story of Job in the Bible is an example of this. Job suffered deeply—he lost his family, fortune, reputation, and health—but in the end, he submitted himself to God's wisdom and the Scriptures tell us, "The LORD blessed the latter days of Job more than his beginning" (Job 42:12). Job's family, fortune, and health were restored, and he lived after his time of suffering one hundred and forty years and "saw his children and grandchildren for four generations" (Job 42:16)!

If we choose to follow God's wisdom in times of difficulty, we will win every time. We may experience material, financial, or relational loss—and even experience death—but what we gain on the other side of life's trials is far better than anything we may have lost if we are trusting the Holy Spirit to impart His wisdom to us. If we die following God's wisdom, we gain the rewards that go to martyrs. If we remain obedient in the trial and do not die, we are often rewarded in extremely generous ways.

We come out deeper in our faith, stronger in our confidence in the Lord, bolder in our witness, and freer in our spirits. If we choose to pursue wisdom no matter how dire the situation we face, we will benefit from the persecution, suffering, or hardship. God will use that experience in our lives to refine us, strengthen us, and bring us to wholeness. He will use it to conform us more to the likeness of Christ Jesus. You can count on it (Rom. 8:29).

GOD'S WISDOM: GOD'S WAY IS HIGHER THAN MAN'S WAY

Earthly wisdom is rooted in the belief that all of life can be understood, rationalized, and proved scientifically. While I am not at all opposed to science or rational thinking, I am also convinced that God's Word says to us that God moves in ways that are still a mystery to man. Science can never prove what causes a person to fall in love. It can never prove what happens to a person after death. It can never measure the breadth or depth of God's love and mercy. It can never decipher or rationalize fully the impulses that motivate the heart of man. God says plainly in His Word: "My thoughts are not your thoughts, nor are your ways My ways . . . For as the heavens are higher than the earth, so are My ways higher than your ways" (Isa. 55:8–9).

The apostle Paul was a powerful debater. He seemed to delight in engaging in controversial discussions with those who did not believe in Christ Jesus. He prompted them to think, to see things differently, and to confront the challenge of the gospel. He wrote this to the Corinthians:

> For the message of the cross is foolishness to those who are perishing, but to us who are being saved it is the power of God. For it is written:

"I will destroy the wisdom of the wise,

And bring to nothing the understanding of the prudent."

(1 Cor. 1:18–19)

Paul knew that to the unbelievers in the Greek world the message of salvation appeared foolish. They could not fathom that a Jewish carpenter and teacher could be crucified on a Roman cross, die, be buried, and then rise from the dead for a divine purpose. They could not comprehend that God might sacrifice His own Son so that sinful mankind might have an opportunity to experience forgiveness and reconciliation with Him. It was not within the realm of their understanding that Christ ascended to heaven and would one day return.

If you totally take God out of your life, the message of the gospel does not make sense. On the other hand, once you have received Jesus Christ as your personal Savior, the gospel makes perfect sense.

Furthermore, God says that one day all the wisdom of the so-called wise and prudent people on this earth will be destroyed. It will come to naught. None of the facts, concepts, principles, or procedures that we have learned about this natural world or human nature will be necessary in eternity. None of the world's information we have acquired or the tangible skills we have developed in order to acquire, maintain, and advance our lives on this earth will be useful in eternity. The wisdom of this world has no capability to carry a person from this life into the next.

Paul went on to write to the Corinthians:

> Where is the wise? Where is the scribe? Where is the
> disputer of this age? Has not God made foolish the wis-
> dom of this world? For since, in the wisdom of God, the
> world through wisdom did not know God, it pleased God
> through the foolishness of the message preached to save
> those who believe. (1 Cor. 1:20–21)

No person in the history of the world has come to a saving
knowledge of God through his or her own intellectual pursuits
or good works. The Bible is very clear on that point. God
reveals Himself to man, imparts the faith to believe in Christ
Jesus, and counts our faith as being all that is necessary for salvation (see Eph. 2:8–9).

Paul concluded:

> For Jews request a sign, and Greeks seek after wisdom;
> but we preach Christ crucified, to the Jews a stumbling
> block and to the Greeks foolishness, but to those who are
> called, both Jews and Greeks, Christ the power of God
> and the wisdom of God. Because the foolishness of God
> is wiser than men, and the weakness of God is stronger
> than men. (1 Cor. 1:22–25)

For the Jews, religion was about God revealing Himself to
His people in miracles, signs, and wonders. For the Greeks,
religion was something intellectual and mental—it was philosophy. But neither miracles nor philosophy resulted in a person's being saved from the consequences of personal sins or

restored to intimate fellowship with God. God had to send His only begotten Son to this earth to die on the cross as the one definitive, atoning, and final sacrifice necessary to take away the sins of mankind.

It makes no sense to an unbeliever that God's Son would have to die a cruel and ignoble death—complete with public shame—so we might one day be resurrected from the dead and live eternally.

It makes no sense to a non-Christian to believe that Jesus Christ is the only way to experience complete pardon from all sin's guilt and shame, to receive eternal life, and to know God fully.

It makes no sense to the person functioning in earthly wisdom that God would require a change of heart in mankind, as opposed to a change in behavior or thinking, and that only the indwelling presence of the Holy Spirit might bring about a genuine heart change.

But, the apostle Paul proclaimed, that's the method God chose! Who has the authority and privilege to choose the method? God does. Who has the power to make judgments based upon His prescribed method? God does. Who has the wisdom to do what is right for man and for accomplishing His purposes on this earth? God does!

Apart from Christianity, every other religion on this earth has a system for how man might achieve righteousness or spiritual enlightenment in his own strength, power, and intellect. Every other religion has a set of rituals or rules that must be followed for a person to arrive at a state of being righteous or holy.

Every other religion presents a spiritual goal that is reached by how much a person does, how much a person gives, how hard a person works, how often a person keeps the rituals, and how deeply a person believes that his works and worship will be sufficient. There is no confidence of a relationship with God, inner peace, or assurance of eternal life.

Only in Christianity has God manifested Himself in human flesh—in the incarnate Jesus, who was born of a virgin, lived a fully human and natural life, and died a physical death hung between two thieves.

Only in Christianity has God reached all the way down to man and said, in effect, "All that I require of you is that you believe in My Son, Jesus Christ, and you shall have the gift of eternal life" (John 3:16).

Only in Christianity has God said, "I'll do all the work—all the dying, sacrifice, ritual, saving, regenerating, renewing—and all that I ask is that you receive what I have done and what I offer to you as being personally applicable to your own life."

To the natural man, steeped in his pride and arrogance, it seems too easy simply to "believe and be saved." To the natural man, who desires to earn and achieve something that makes him feel more important, it seems too humbling to "bow" before God and "be set free from sin's dominion."

To the natural man, God should have set His Son on a throne, not a cross. To the natural man, God should have given His Son long life, not three short years of ministry and then death. To the natural man, God should have inspired His Son to write a doctrinal statement, a book of rules, or a curriculum to study and memorize, not to preach a simple message: "Believe and receive."

Nevertheless, as foolish as it may seem to the unredeemed man, God has chosen to reveal His power and His wisdom through Christ. Where man's understanding ends, God's wisdom begins. Where man's power ends, God's power takes over. God is the One in control—not only of all things in this natural world, the political world, and the course of history and human events. He is in control of all things in the spiritual realm as well! God is the One who has all authority, power, and wisdom to set the rules, establish the process that results in forgiveness and the granting of eternal life, and give spiritual gifts to mankind.

GOD'S WISDOM: WHAT WORKS BEST IS GOD'S WAY

Earthly wisdom proclaims: "Do what works." Generally speaking, what works is regarded as what makes the most money or brings fame and power. Unfortunately, we have thousands of examples all around us of moral failure in the wake of "what works."

Look at what has happened in the entertainment industry in just the last fifty years. Television programs, music recordings, movies, video games, theatrical shows, and live concerts—all have become increasingly sensual, increasingly explicit in presenting sexual behavior, increasingly violent, and increasingly reliant upon special effects that present a fantasy world. The entertainment world has also become increasingly occult, with more and more themes involving horror, paranormal phenomena, supernatural creatures, demonic powers, and forces for evil. Today's entertainment messages are a reflection of man's rabid appetite for things that are more and more sensual, more and more powerful, and more and more "otherworldly." They are perhaps the ultimate example in our world today of earthly wisdom.

These messages seem to work because they make money and catapult people to fame. But what is working at the moral or spiritual level? Nothing is working to bring people the things that money cannot buy and that every person ultimately wants: love, worthiness, fulfillment, joy, peace, and an assurance of eternal life. God's wisdom proclaims: Only God's way really works.

EARTHLY WISDOM AND GODLY WISDOM PRODUCE DIFFERENT OUTCOMES

Take a look at the end results of earthly wisdom and godly wisdom. They are very different. Earthly wisdom produces in the human heart, and in human relationships, very different fruit from that produced by godly wisdom. Read what James wrote about this:

> Who is wise and understanding among you? Let him show by good conduct that his works are done in the meekness of wisdom. But if you have bitter envy and self-seeking in your hearts, do not boast and lie against the truth. This wisdom does not descend from above, but is

earthly, sensual, and demonic. For where envy and self-seeking exist, confusion and every evil thing are there. But the wisdom that is from above is first pure, then peaceable, gentle, willing to yield, full of mercy and good fruits, without partiality and without hypocrisy. Now the fruit of righteousness is sown in peace by those who make peace. (James 3:13–18)

What a sharp contrast between earthly wisdom and godly wisdom! The contrast is drawn on the basis of results:

- Earthly wisdom results in power struggles, personal kingdom building, greed, envy, avarice, and an argumentative spirit. As James wrote, earthly wisdom is "self-seeking."

- Earthly wisdom results in a deep drive to satisfy human cravings and lust. It results in addictions, obsessions, and, ultimately, confusion about what is morally right and wrong.

- Earthly wisdom is under the influence of the evil one. It results in blasphemy, heresy, self-justification for sin, and spiritual error.

John wrote in his first epistle: "For all that is in the world—the lust of the flesh, the lust of the eyes, and the pride of life—is not of the Father but is of the world. And the world is passing away, and the lust of it; but he who does the will of God abides forever" (1 John 2:16–17).

The concepts are the same. The "lust of the flesh" refers to those things that are sensual. The "lust of the eyes" refers to those things that are rooted in pride, greed, and a hunger for personal power and recognition. The "pride of life" refers to man's desire to be number one and to exert his will and authority rather than yield to God's authority.

If you question whether something is rooted in earthly wisdom or divine wisdom, take a look at the outcome! Take a look at the fruit. Those things that are rooted in earthly wisdom result in people being at odds with one another, confusion about what is right and wrong, and all forms of evil behavior.

And what about divine wisdom? Godly wisdom is marked by . . .

- *purity.* God's wisdom produces behavior that is morally pure, chaste, and modest.

- *peace.* God's wisdom produces relationship, not estrangement.

- *gentleness.* God's wisdom does not demand its own way but rather functions by influence. It comforts even as it counsels, offers hope even as it convicts, and leads rather than forces a person to God.

- *a willingness to yield self.* God's wisdom is not rooted in pride but rather in service. The person functioning according to godly wisdom will do all he can to help others, to minister to others, to consider others, to bless others, and to care for others.

- *mercy and good fruits.* God's wisdom is marked by kindness, generosity, and helpfulness. Those who walk wisely are givers, not grasping takers.

Furthermore, these outcomes of divine wisdom function . . .

- *without partiality.* God's wisdom operates without prejudice against another person's race, color, background, social standing, economic level, culture, age, or gender.

- *without hypocrisy.* When divine wisdom is at work, there is consistency in what a person believes, says, and does—there are integrity, honesty, and transparency.

Earthly wisdom is limited by man's ability to perceive, to sense, to learn, to understand, to create, and to control. Earthly wisdom is "doing what comes naturally"—and what comes naturally to unredeemed mankind is what satisfies the senses, feeds human pride, and fosters greed. Earthly wisdom can never rise above man's fallen nature.

Godly wisdom is marked by God's ability to work through mankind. As Paul proclaimed, "I can do all things through Christ who strengthens me" (Phil. 4:13). When we allow God to work in us and through us, our abilities to perceive, to sense, to learn, to understand, to create, and to manage life's resources are powerfully expanded.

Godly wisdom is doing what the Holy Spirit compels us to do. It results in what is pleasing to God and ultimately, what is beneficial to man.

Godly wisdom calls a man to rise above his own nature and function according to the indwelling presence and power of the Holy Spirit—not that man might be equal to God, but that man might be a vessel used by God to bring blessing to this earth.

WE MUST CHOOSE GOD'S WISDOM

God's wisdom is not foisted on us. We must choose wisdom. We must invite God to lead us to His way and His plan. We must ask ourselves continually:

- Is this a wise decision?

- Is this a wise use of my talents, gifts, skills, or resources?

- Is this a wise action to take in a relationship?

- Is this a wise way to live out the purpose God has for my life?

As we ask these questions, we must look and listen for God's response. We must ask for God's wisdom with a prayer, "Lord, give me Your answer."

THREE

EIGHT AMAZINGLY WONDERFUL
BENEFITS OF WISDOM

A person who applies for a job in today's marketplace is generally concerned with not only the job description and salary but the benefits provided by the employer as well. People are concerned with what they are going to receive in exchange for the effort, skills, and creativity they provide. It's a good concern to have.

Have you ever asked a similar question about the benefits that come from following Jesus Christ? God's benefit plan is absolutely fantastic! Those who accept Christ Jesus as their personal Savior receive two tremendous benefits: forgiveness of sin and eternal life. You can't beat those benefits!

The daily benefits of following Christ are also tremendous—guidance, provision, protection, comfort, help in resolving life's problems, and an outpouring of God's presence.

Have you ever asked specifically, "What are the benefits of seeking God's wisdom?" God's Word gives a very clear answer. Wisdom yields eight truly amazing and wonderful benefits!

BENEFIT #1: A GAIN IN ONE'S KNOWLEDGE OF GOD

The supreme benefit to those who walk in godly wisdom is that they grow in their knowledge of God. We read in Proverbs:

> If you seek her [wisdom] as silver,
> And search for her as for hidden treasures;
> Then you will understand the fear of the LORD,
> And find the knowledge of God. (Prov. 2:4–5)

Reflect upon the last twenty-four hours of your life. How did God work in you, through you, and around you in the lives of others? What did God reveal to you about Himself, about your own self, about your relationship with Him, and about your relationships with other people?

In what ways did you find yourself responding or acting in accordance with God's Word? Do you feel convicted in your spirit about your responses to situations or people that were not in keeping with God's commandments and principles? In what ways do you feel your attitude or behavior could have been more like that of Christ Jesus?

The person who is seeking to walk in wisdom is going to reflect often about his own relationship with the Lord and how the Lord desires to work in his life. He is going to want to please the Lord, to grow in his relationship with the Lord, and to experience a presence of the Lord at all times.

As we walk in wisdom, we see God's hand at every turn. We

know He is with us. We become more and more familiar with His voice . . . His prompting . . . His leading . . . His tug at our hearts. We don't merely know more about God—rather, we truly come to know God in a deeper and more intimate way.

The more we come to know God, the more we are going to learn the way God works, the things God desires to do in our lives and in the lives of others, and the plans God has made for mankind's eternal good. We are going to feel God's heartbeat. What disappoints God is going to disappoint us. What brings joy to heaven is going to bring joy to us. What brings concern to the Lord is going to concern us. We are going to see things from God's perspective, and we are going to grow in our desire to love others as God loves them.

As we grow in our knowledge of God and His ways, the more we are going to know how much God loves us, how much He desires to bless us, and how much He desires to use us to bless others.

I assure you of this—when you truly catch a glimpse of how much God loves you and desires to work all things in this life to your eternal benefit, you are going to feel incredibly, wonderfully blessed! Knowledge of God is a tremendous benefit.

BENEFIT #2: CLEAR GUIDANCE FROM GOD

Those who walk in wisdom receive God's clear direction for their lives. They are spared many mistakes and false starts. They are kept from making wrong decisions or entering into hurtful relationships. They take fewer detours in life and experience fewer obstacles in their path.

Never lose sight of the fact that God sees the totality of your life. He knows you inside and out. He knows your thoughts, your feelings, your physical makeup. He knows your past, your present, and your future. He knows your natural talents, your experiences, your spiritual gifts. God sees the whole of who you are, what you are called to do, and what you are facing right now. The more you see your life from God's perspective, the stronger your ability to discern the right way to go.

Not only does God know you thoroughly, but He also knows what He desires to do in you and through you. He knows precisely the next move you should make, the next words you should speak, and the next encounter you will have.

There is nobody better qualified than God to guide your steps or to lead you into right paths. The Scriptures tell us:

> Hear, my son, and receive my sayings,
> And the years of your life will be many.
> I have taught you in the way of wisdom;
> I have led you in right paths.
> When you walk, your steps will not be hindered,
> And when you run, you will not stumble. (Prov 4:10–12)

What a joy to walk into God's destiny for you and not be tripped up, held back, pushed down, or hindered in any way! What a joy to run toward the fulfillment of God's purpose for your life and never fall or stumble!

God's desire is to guard us and guide us every step and every hour of every day.

WHEN WE IGNORE GOD'S GUIDANCE

Plain and simple, those who willfully reject or ignore God's guidance are headed for trouble. They are also headed for God's discipline. Proverbs 10:13 warns, "A rod is for the back of him who is devoid of understanding." Chastisement awaits those who reject God's direction.

Why does God chastise His people? To bring them back into a position where He can bless them! God does not delight in chastisement. He is not a punitive, abusive God. God chastises His people to correct them so they will not experience the full consequences of their rebellion, sin, or error. His love for us and His desire to bless us compel Him to take action to keep us from our own self-destruction.

Proverbs 10:14 gives a slightly different warning, "The mouth of the foolish is near destruction." Those who speak earthly wisdom and ignore God's guidance in their speech are going to self-destruct. Their words will bring them to harm. God chastises us to keep us from saying things that will come back to haunt us, hurt us, or hinder us. Proverbs 3:5–6 gives us this wonderful promise:

> Trust in the LORD with all your heart,
> And lean not on your own understanding;
> In all your ways acknowledge Him,
> And He shall direct your paths.

To direct your path means that He will make your way smooth or straight. In other words, God will clear the way for you. He will give you guidance that you clearly recognize and clearly understand. God's Word also says,

> My son, let them not depart from your eyes—
> Keep sound wisdom and discretion;
> So they will be life to your soul
> And grace to your neck.
> Then you will walk safely in your way,
> And your foot will not stumble.
> When you lie down, you will not be afraid;
> Yes, you will lie down and your sleep will be sweet.
> Do not be afraid of sudden terror,
> Nor of trouble from the wicked when it comes;
> For the LORD will be your confidence,
> And will keep your foot from being caught.
> (Prov. 3:21–26)

The Lord imparts to us an abiding feeling of security and confidence. The Lord's guidance leads us to live without fear, even to the point where we can sleep soundly and deeply. How many people do you know today—and you may even be one of them—who are awake part of every night worrying about what the next day will bring or second-guessing events of the previous day? As we follow God's wisdom, He frees us from anxiety—we can rest assured that He has the power to fix, to heal, or to mend anything that may go awry in our lives.

When we seek to walk in divine wisdom, we can rest assured that the Lord is with us always. He will not allow us to enter into any situation or circumstance that He has not anticipated or intends to use for our good.

BENEFIT #3: GOD'S DIVINE PROTECTION

When we walk in divine wisdom, we experience God's protection from evil. Very specifically, God's wisdom serves to protect us from evil, from people who entice us to engage in evil, from making serious mistakes, and from relying on capricious emotions.

EVIL

God desires to protect us from all things that are evil—from substances that do us harm, from situations that are dangerous, from environments that are deadly, from circumstances that can destroy us. God's wisdom leads us as far away from evil as possible.

Many people seem to enjoy walking as close to the edge as they can. They want to partake of as much of the world as possible without actually entering into deep sin. They flirt with evil, thinking perhaps that this makes life more interesting, fun, or exciting. God's Word, however, calls us to live as far away from evil as possible. We are to run from evil, to flee from it, to reject it completely, and to avoid it whenever possible. God's Word says,

> The simple believes every word,
> But the prudent considers well his steps.

A wise man fears and departs from evil,

But a fool rages and is self-confident. (Prov. 14:15−16)

PEOPLE WHO ENTICE US TO ENGAGE IN EVIL

At times we are tempted directly by evil, but at other times, we are tempted by people who entice us to participate in evil activities or go to places where evil abounds. Any person who entices you to sin is not a friend. That person should be considered an enemy because he is attempting to lead you into a situation that will ultimately cause you loss or harm.

I have met people who seem drawn to evil people—they find them interesting, exciting, intriguing. They actively seek out those who live on the "wild side" or who are engaged in sin, often because they secretly desire to experience sin vicariously. God's wisdom is that we avoid people we know to be evil. Don't spend time with them, listen to them, laugh at their jokes, take their advice, enter into flirtatious conversation with them, or seek to cultivate their friendship. God's Word is very clear on this:

When wisdom enters your heart,

And knowledge is pleasant to your soul,

Discretion will preserve you;

Understanding will keep you,

To deliver you from the way of evil,

From the man who speaks perverse things,

From those who leave the paths of uprightness

To walk in the ways of darkness;

Who rejoice in doing evil,

And delight in the perversity of the wicked;
Whose ways are crooked,
And who are devious in their paths;
To deliver you from the immoral woman,
From the seductress who flatters with her words,
Who forsakes the companion of her youth,
And forgets the covenant of her God.
For her house leads down to death,
And her paths to the dead. (Prov. 2:10–18)

SERIOUS MISTAKES

Most of us make mistakes because we do not know the right choice or decision to make. We do not consciously say, "I am now going to make a mistake." Rather, we tend to make mistakes by being careless regarding the needs or desires of others, by not asking the right questions, or by not taking into consideration all the factors that are important to consider.

Most of the time our mistakes do not affect us alone. Others are nearly always involved. In fact, we tend to know we have made a mistake because somebody else tells us so! When we seek God's wisdom, He leads us to decisions that are right, just, equitable, and good not only for us personally, but for everybody involved. God's Word says,

He guards the paths of justice,
And preserves the way of His saints.

Then you will understand righteousness and justice,
Equity and every good path. (Prov. 2:8–9)

CAPRICIOUS EMOTIONS

Many people today walk according to how they feel in any given moment. They live their lives out of their emotions. The problem with emotions is that they come and go. A person can be happy one day and sad the next. A person can feel one way about a person, situation, or decision one week, and a very different way the next week. Those who live on an emotional roller coaster often find themselves veering into calamity. And those who live with a person who rides an emotional roller coaster often live in a state of frustration!

The Bible tells us that the heart of man is deceitful and wicked (Jer. 17:9). Left to our own devices, we tend to lie to ourselves—we deceive ourselves into hearing what we want to hear, doing what is pleasing to our senses, and pursuing what gives us a happy feeling.

In the pursuit of what people think will give them the positive emotions of peace, joy, and love, they often find themselves going places, doing things, and partaking of substances that, in the end, provide anything but lasting peace, joy, and love. There's nothing joyful about a house of prostitution, a place where drugs are being consumed or alcohol is being consumed in large quantity, a place where crime is being planned, or a place where people are angry, rebellious, or out of control.

When we seek to live according to God's wisdom, we are saying to our emotions: "I walk by faith, not by sight. I will not base every decision on the way that I feel—or the way that I think a certain decision will cause me to feel. I will walk by what the Word of God says. I am going to trust the Holy Spirit to guide me, not my own desires, impulses, and emotions."

Please understand that I am not opposed to emotions. God made us with emotions, and they have a good and rightful place in our lives. God gave us emotions to motivate us to take action, to right the wrongs we see, to express our delight and joy at His work in our lives, and to release tension and stress. But God never intended for us to live out of our emotions— He intends for us to live out of a will that is subjected to His will for us.

Emotions tend to run hot or cold. Blazing-hot emotions readily lead to anger, which can lead to arguments and conflicts that run the gamut from abuse to neighborhood gang fights to international war. Ice-cold emotions create an environment filled with tension, estrangement, and very often bitterness and hatred.

In contrast to living by emotions, those who live according to God's wisdom find themselves reaching out in love to others—not because they always feel love, or feel like giving, but because they are living in obedience to God's command to love others. Loving words and actions produce relationship, friendship, camaraderie, and high morale—all of which are evidence of mutual support. Those who have a circle of loving family members and friends feel secure, safe, and protected. Not only do they feel that way, they *are* secure, safe, and protected.

What is true for our human relationships is also true for our relationship with the Lord. When we lay down any hot anger we have against God . . . when we lay down our feelings of estrangement or bitterness against God . . . and when we choose to receive the Lord into our lives and live according to His loving commandments and principles . . . we experience God's security, safety, and protection. The Lord becomes our rock, our fortress, our safe haven, and our shelter in the time of storm.

God's Word admonishes us:

Get wisdom! Get understanding!
Do not forget, nor turn away from the words of my mouth.
Do not forsake her [wisdom], and she will preserve you;
Love her, and she will keep you. (Prov. 4:5–6)

He who trusts in his own heart is a fool,
But whoever walks wisely will be delivered. (Prov. 28:26)

Let me give you an example of these first three benefits in action. I recently encountered a young man whose wife had abandoned their relationship. She had left suddenly and in a hurtful way, emptying their joint bank account and accusing him of violence and abuse—accusations that were unfounded. In reality, the violence and abuse she had experienced in her life were from her childhood and previous relationships. She, herself, tended to be the violent abuser.

This woman lived out of her emotions. One day she was "up," the next "down." One day she was loving, the next day angry. No sooner had she left their home than trouble began in her life. She found herself depressed, anxious, and fearful. She began to seek solace in bars, which was something she had not done for a number of years. She went through thousands of dollars in a matter of weeks, driving thousands of miles from home and spending money on things that she frantically hoped would give her self-worth, but that in the end, left her on the brink of exhaustion and poverty.

Her phone calls back to her husband were filled with obscene language but also expressions of confusion. She frequently said, "I don't know what to do. I don't know where to turn." And of course, she said it was all his fault.

I asked this young man what he was doing in response to her absence and her accusations. He replied very simply, "I'm burrowing into God."

"Burrowing into God?" I asked.

"Yes," he said. "I'm digging even deeper into God's Word. I'm spending even more time in prayer. I'm seeking wise counsel in a way that I've never humbled myself to seek it before. I'm staying in close fellowship with my godly friends."

"And what is the result?" I asked.

"The result has been amazing. My heart has been at peace. I go to bed at night in peace and wake up in peace. I feel God's protection all around me. I had to go to court a few weeks ago, and I was afraid of what might happen, especially since my wife was accusing me of all sorts of abuse that simply never happened in our relationship. The judge called a lunch recess between her testimony and the time I was to take the stand. I spent much of that lunch hour in prayer. And when we returned to the courthouse, suddenly her attorney asked for reconciliation! All of the abuse charges against me were dropped, and I never did have to take the stand."

"Do you feel God guiding you?" I asked.

"Absolutely. He hasn't told me fully what I am to do, but He has shown me the right steps to take as I face each crisis point. He has given me the courage to require that my wife get godly counseling before we live under the same roof again. He has led me to require a full accounting of the funds that were taken. He has shown me that He will be the One who brings healing to each of us individually."

"And what have you learned about God in all this?" I asked.

"He's there. I can count on that. He's right there." As this young man voiced those words, his eyes welled with tears. "God has never felt closer than in the last three months."

Was this young man walking in wisdom? Yes. And in the process, he was growing in his knowledge of God—he was experiencing God's love, tender mercy, and abiding presence. He was receiving clear guidance from the Lord. And he was being protected mightily.

BENEFIT #4: GOD'S STRENGTH AND POWER

When we seek divine wisdom, God imparts to us the ability to see a situation from His perspective, which is this: He has strength and ability to compensate for every area of weakness we have. He enables us to do what we cannot do in our own strength.

The person who is walking wisely comes to the conclusion: "There's nothing too big . . . too difficult . . . too problematic for God to handle." Problems to us may seem as big as a mountain, but from God's perspective, the same problems are lighter than a feather. God's Word assures us:

A wise man is strong,
Yes, a man of knowledge increases strength;
For by wise counsel you will wage your own war,
And in a multitude of counselors there is safety. (Prov. 24:5–6)

What does it mean to "wage your own war"? We must recognize that the enemy of our souls is lurking behind every serious trouble or trial we face. I'm not saying that the devil causes every problem we face—some of our problems are due to our own rebellion, error, or sin. Nevertheless, the devil stands ready in any problem or difficulty to take full advantage of the situation. If we give him even the slightest crack in the door, he will come roaring through it with a vengeance! The devil pounces on every opportunity given to him to kill, destroy, and steal from us (John 10:10).

The devil is intent on robbing our integrity, destroying our witness for Christ Jesus, stealing our possessions, hindering our relationship with Christ, killing the love in our family relationships and friendships, tearing apart our churches and ministry organizations, and stealing our health. Our battle is with him. And it is only as we acquire godly wisdom that we recognize this fact and learn how to wage spiritual warfare against him. It is as we acquire wisdom that we know what to say, how to pray, what to do, and when to act to defeat the devil at every turn and emerge victorious against him.

There is a big difference between those who see life as a war they are waging successfully and those who see life as a war they are losing. Many people see life as being extremely hard— they have very little hope that things can be better or easier. They struggle just to maintain emotional equilibrium and the status quo. They have very little hope, contentment, or joy because they carry the full burden of their own lives. They have internalized enough strife and stress to give them a nervous breakdown at any hour of a twenty-four-hour day.

When a person believes that he does not live his life solely in his own strength, but that he lives and moves and has his being in Christ, then he has the confidence within that he has a divine ally with him always. He has a knowing deep within that what he cannot do in his own physical strength, Christ can energize him to do. What he cannot know in his own mental strength, Christ can impart to him from His infinite wisdom. What he cannot accomplish by his own abilities, Christ can accomplish through His divine enabling, guiding, guarding power.

BENEFIT #5: GENUINE JOY AND CONTENTMENT

Again and again, I encounter people who have very little peace, contentment, or happiness in their lives. They seem continually to be striving against something. They have an angry, fighting spirit—there always seems to be something wrong that they are attempting to right through their own ideas, power, or energy. They don't just walk down a hallway . . . they march at double time. They can't sit down and relax . . . they sit at the edge of their chair, poised to jump up and do something. They don't allow themselves the so-called luxury of spending time just meditating about the Lord . . . they must be doing something that they believe is vitally important—puttering around, shuffling paper, working on a project. Many times, they feel tremendous guilt if they take only five minutes to do nothing.

People who live striving lives tend to be people who believe they are unworthy before God or others. They believe they must produce a string of good works, accomplishments, rewards, awards, or completed tasks to show for their time and effort in order for their lives to have value or meaning.

Let me assure you of this: Striving will never result in your salvation. Good works count for nothing in God's eyes. It is only our faith—our simply believing—in Jesus Christ that results in our salvation. No amount of striving will result in your receiving or living in the power of the Holy Spirit. The Holy Spirit is God's automatic gift to your life the moment you believe and receive Jesus Christ as your Savior. Neither does striving produce the inner quality that God desires to see in each of us: trust in Him.

Let me also assure you of this: Continually striving against someone or something causes joy, peace, and contentment to drain from your being. It saps energy. It produces a constant feeling of inner exhaustion, which can in turn produce feelings of depression and discouragement. God's Word declares,

Happy is the man who finds wisdom . . .

Her ways are ways of pleasantness,

And all her paths are peace.

She is a tree of life to those who take hold of her,

And happy are all who retain her. (Prov. 3:13, 17–18)

God's Word clearly tells us that those who walk wisely will experience "pleasantness," peace, and happiness. Wisdom is likened to a tree—a living, long-lasting shelter that provides a place of inner rest against life's storms and the heat of life's troubles.

Can a person live in joy, peace, and contentment every second of every day throughout life? No. Moments of panic, fear, discouragement, sadness, disappointment, or pain hit all of us from time to time. But, joy, peace, and contentment can characterize the whole of your life. They can be the hallmarks of your attitude, your mood, and your outlook.

Recall our definition of *wisdom*: "Wisdom is the capacity to see things from God's perspective and to respond to them according to scriptural principles." When a person faces a difficulty that seems to rob him of peace, joy, or contentment, the wisdom of God reminds that person:

- God loves me unconditionally.

- God is in control.

- God has a reason for allowing this in my life.

- God is walking through this difficult time with me.

When we know with certainty that God is in control, that He loves us beyond measure, and that He is at work in our lives, we have the genuine capacity to praise and thank God even in the midst of the most dire, discouraging, or depressing times. And our praise and thanksgiving create in us very live feelings of joy and peace.

Take a look for just a moment at what causes frustration, anxiety, and worry. Those who are without God, or who are rejecting God's wisdom, can't help but feel anxious because from their perspective, life is out of control and marked by chaos; void of love; lived moment to moment, feeling to feeling; and solitary.

What a terrible way to live! Even if these beliefs aren't carried to the extreme, they are beliefs that can weigh a person down. Believing with the whole heart that God is in control brings us peace. Believing with the whole heart that God loves us and is working for our good brings us joy. Believing with the whole heart that God is with us every moment of every day brings us contentment.

What awesome assurance that our God is sufficient in all times, for all circumstances! The One who governs and guards is the One who gives us joy, peace, and happiness.

BENEFIT #6: A GOOD SELF-IMAGE

I am always amazed at the number of books that continue to be published and the number of seminars that continue to be held on the topic of self-esteem. I can only conclude that so much self-esteem material continues to be produced because many people are struggling with a poor self-image. The reason for the poor self-image is ultimately that people do not see themselves as being valuable, worthy, or acceptable to God.

When a person knows he is of extreme importance to God, and God loves him, values him, and desires to be in close relationship with him, that person has confidence and a strong self-image.

Take a look at the five benefits of wisdom we have already covered in this chapter:

- A deeper knowledge of God
- Clear guidance from God
- Protection by God
- Strength and power from God
- Joy and contentment

Now let me ask you: If you truly believe you are associated with God who reveals Himself to you, guides you daily, protects you always, gives you strength and power to make it through every day with hope and courage, and imparts to you joy and contentment, how can you have a poor self-image? The almighty, awesome God of the universe is your heavenly Father! He is not only your Creator but also your Sustainer, Provider, Protector, and Lover of your soul forever. You are His child, and you will live with Him forever.

How can a poor self-image thrive in the face of such beliefs? The wisdom of God leads us to see ourselves as God sees us, not as the world defines us, people in our past have defined us, or even as we have come to define ourselves. The wisdom of God presents to us the image of a person who is a joint heir of Christ Jesus. God's Word tells us:

> Now therefore, listen to me, my children,
> For blessed are those who keep my ways.
> Hear instruction and be wise,
> And do not disdain it.
> Blessed is the man who listens to me,
> Watching daily at my gates,
> Waiting at the posts of my doors.
> For whoever finds me finds life,
> And obtains favor from the LORD. (Prov. 8:32–35)

Note that the person who seeks godly wisdom is "blessed." He is in a position to receive the overflowing abundance of God's goodness. He is also the person who "obtains favor" from the Lord. If God is blessing us, and we have the favor—the approval—of the Lord, how can we have a poor self-image?

If you genuinely believe that God desires to bless you and that He approves of you and loves you unconditionally, you must ask yourself, "On what is my poor self-image based?" You're going to have to draw your own conclusions—your poor self-image comes from lies of the enemy or lies from other people. And you must take responsibility for the fact that you have bought into those lies and continue to accept them as truth.

The devil will lie to you continually, telling you that God doesn't love you, you aren't saved by Jesus Christ, you are still in bondage to sin, or you aren't worthy of His blessings.

Other people lie to you also—perhaps not intentionally, but nonetheless, they do not speak God's truth to you. They tell you that you can never be a person of accomplishment, worth, or acceptance, even though God's Word says otherwise.

The world at large—especially the entertainment media—will tell you that unless you look a certain way, dress a certain way, own certain objects, or achieve certain levels of social status, you will forever be unlovable or a second-class person.

Have you bought into these lies?

The person who seeks godly wisdom comes to believe, "I am blessed by God. God loves me and approves of me. I am saved by the blood of Jesus Christ, filled with God's Spirit, and on the basis of what Jesus has done for me and the Holy Spirit continues to do in me, I have favor from God. All of God's promises pertain to me. All of the talents that God has built into my life are worthy to be developed and used. God has a plan for my life that He is unfolding. God is refining me, preparing me, and molding me into the likeness of Christ Jesus. I belong to Him forever, and He is my loving Father who is continually seeking my good."

Believe that . . . and you will have a good and proper self-image!

EMBRACE GOD'S LOVE FOR YOU

At the very core of our self-image is the desire to be loved and to be regarded as lovable. Only God can fully satisfy that need. When we truly come to believe that God loves us and deems us worthy of His unconditional love, we have the foundation for a healthy, godly self-esteem.

Throughout the years, and not only in the United States but in nations around the world, I have found the most difficult truth for Christian people to believe is this: God loves me unconditionally. I receive letters from time to time that say, "I don't believe that God can continue to love me after the way I have sinned or strayed from His plan for my life."

Let me ask you, Have you placed conditions on God's love? What are they? Some of the most common conditions that Christian believers place on God seem to be these:

- "I have sinned . . . so God can't love me." God's Word says, "God demonstrates His own love toward us, in that while we were still sinners, Christ died for us" (Rom. 5:8). God loved you even before you accepted Him. He loved you first and He loves you always. He desires for you to repent of your sin and be forgiven, to change your ways and grow in Christ . . . but His love for you is unwavering.

- "I haven't done enough to warrant God's love." No person can earn God's love. God loves us from His own divine motivation. His love for us is never "awarded" to us on the basis of our good works. Everything we receive from God is something that God has already made available to us free of charge, free of effort, free of striving. You cannot "earn" God's peace. You cannot "achieve" enough points for God to give you joy. You cannot "win" God's love.

We read in 1 John 4:19, "We love Him because He first loved us." God is continually reaching out to us in love, not because of anything we initiate or do, but because He has chosen from ages past to love us, pursue us, forgive us, and conform us into the image of His Son, Jesus Christ.

If you believe that your sin or your failure keeps God from loving you, you need to face up to the fact that you are the one who is placing conditions on God's love. God hasn't placed conditions on His love . . . you have!

THE VALUE OF GODLY SELF-ESTEEM

Some people don't seem to believe that a good self-image is something godly people should have. The Word of God says, "He who gets wisdom loves his own soul" (Prov. 19:8). That's as clear as A, B, C! Those who walk in wisdom see themselves as God sees them and they begin to love themselves as God loves them. Jesus said, "You shall love your neighbor as *yourself*" (Matt. 22:39, emphasis added). You cannot love others unless you have a love for yourself that is rooted in God's love for you. A proper, healthy love for one's self leads a person to be generous and giving toward others. The person who walks wisely knows that God has loved him even though he did nothing to deserve that love, and therefore, he is much more likely to reach out with love to others even though they may have done nothing to deserve his love.

A godly self-esteem not only gives us a strengthened capacity to love and to forgive others, but it gives us boldness in moving against the tide of popular opinion. If you know with assurance that you have God's love and His favor on your life, it doesn't matter to you if a person criticizes you, rejects you, or speaks ill of you to others. God loves you and approves of you, and His opinion is the only opinion that matters!

BENEFIT #7: WHOLE-PERSON PROSPERITY

Does God bless those who love and serve Him and walk according to His ways? Absolutely. When you walk in wisdom, you will prosper.

God's prosperity is for the whole person—spirit, mind, and body. The Bible says, "Beloved, I pray that you may prosper in all things and be in health, just as your soul prospers" (3 John 2). That one verse encapsulates the totality of prosperity—prosperity in one's health, in one's soul, and in all things—which includes all relationships, endeavors, investments, and the management of all possessions.

All wealth is certainly not confined to gold, silver, paper money, stocks, bonds, or land. There is much wealth in knowing God, walking in His ways, and experiencing His strength, power, peace, joy, and contentment. Wealth, however, includes material possessions and joyful, delightful experiences that God provides for us as we live on this earth. Read God's counsel:

> I love those who love me,
> And those who seek me diligently will find me.

Riches and honor are with me,

Enduring riches and righteousness.

My fruit is better than gold, yes, than fine gold,

And my revenue than choice silver.

I traverse the way of righteousness,

In the midst of the paths of justice,

That I may cause those who love me to inherit wealth,

That I may fill their treasuries. (Prov. 8:17–21)

Both spiritual and natural "wealth" are described in this passage. God's prosperity certainly focuses on those things of lasting value—the "enduring riches and righteousness." But it also includes "riches and honor"—material wealth as well as rewards and honors that come from other people.

Right standing with God and justice before man are two of the most important things a person might ever have, but this passage speaks in the very next sentence of wealth that is inherited and "treasuries" that are full.

Why does God prosper His people? For one main reason: so that we might be a blessing to others. God does not pour out wealth on people so they might keep what they receive, but rather, so they might be generous givers.

BENEFIT #8: GOOD HEALTH AND A LONG LIFE

No person can promise another person healing from a particular disease or a long life—I certainly will not do that. But read what God's Word says,

> Do not be wise in your own eyes;
> Fear the LORD and depart from evil.
> It will be health to your flesh,
> And strength to your bones. (Prov. 3:7–8)

Health and strength are God's desire for those who walk wisely, fear Him, and run from evil. The godly life is characterized by health and wholeness, and a life of health and wholeness is likely to be a long life.

There are very practical, logical reasons for this. The person who sees his life in the context of God's plan and purpose is going to be a person who values his time and seeks to make the most of every hour God gives him. He is going to plan for good health practices in order to put quality into his life and to add as much quantity to his life as possible. The godly person should desire to live as long as possible in order to do as much as possible to extend the gospel of Jesus Christ. He should seek to use his gifts and talents every day in such a way that God's mercy, forgiveness, and goodness are furthered on this earth.

When you value your time on earth as a servant of God, you are going to want to take care of your body. You are going to seek out God's wisdom about how to eat, how to exercise, how to get sufficient sleep, and how to engage in relaxing activities. You are going to get God's wisdom about how to defeat stress and live in contentment. You are going to fill your day with things that are fruitful and profitable. And as you put God's principles to work in your life, you are going to experience health and strength.

In light of these eight amazingly wonderful benefits of wisdom, why would any person choose to walk in foolishness?

The only reason I can fathom is that a person does not know how to discover and apply God's wisdom. That is where we turn next.

FOUR

The Essentials for Walking in Wisdom

Through the years I have traveled quite a bit in the course of my personal life and ministry. Just recently someone asked me how many cruises I had taken or had sponsored as part of my ministry. I was a bit startled as I added them up— seventy-one! In preaching revivals and holding training conferences for believers, I have logged millions of miles of travel.

One thing I have discovered about travel is that I enjoy planning for a trip as much as I enjoy taking a trip. When I am preparing for a photographic excursion, I take pleasure in laying out all the gear I think I will need. I enjoy the process of determining what I need to leave behind and what are the absolute essentials to make a trip enjoyable and productive. What clothes do I take? What vitamins and supplements do I pack? What emergency items might be useful to have along? Which lenses do I take for which cameras?

The journey of life requires certain essentials. If we are going to walk in wisdom, there are certain things we must do. There are certain ways we need to think and believe, certain actions we need to take if we are going to pursue, acquire, and live in God's wisdom.

ESSENTIAL #1: HAVE STRONG DETERMINATION TO WALK WISELY

The first requirement for walking wisely is to have a strong determination to gain wisdom. Just because a person is a Christian does not mean he has an automatic desire to walk wisely. We must consciously and intentionally decide that we are going to pursue God's wisdom and walk in it.

Those who have the Holy Spirit resident in their spirits do not automatically make wise choices and engage in wise actions. Furthermore, it is one thing to know what to do and another thing to do it. We must consciously and intentionally ask the Holy Spirit to guide us into wisdom and give us the courage to walk in it.

We also face the challenge of making decisions in a wide variety of areas—some decisions involve our health, others involve our work, others involve our family, others involve our handling of material resources or money, and still others involve our personal devotion to the Lord. Each of these areas tends to change over time. Our health is never constant, our work projects change, our family grows and develops, our income or resources may change, and the amount of time we spend with the Lord tends to vary. We continually find ourselves in new situations, facing new circumstances. To walk wisely, we must consciously and intentionally ask the Lord daily to reveal His wisdom in every area of challenge, difficulty, or opportunity we face.

A strong determination to walk wisely comes from having these things settled in our hearts and minds: the assurance of God's omniscience and a firm commitment to do whatever it takes to seek and acquire wisdom.

ASSURANCE OF GOD'S OMNISCIENCE

Do you genuinely believe that whatever God says to you is right, good, true, wise, and for your eternal benefit? Do you have full assurance that knowing God's will, pleasing God, and being conformed to the likeness of Christ Jesus are always God's plan? That walking wisely is the only way to fulfill God's purpose for your life? That the way of foolishness always ends in trouble, difficulty, and sorrow?

I am continually amazed at the number of people who say they believe that God's Word is right, good, true, wise, and always for their benefit—but then they second-guess God and choose to go their own way. Many times they don't openly admit that they believe their way is better than God's way, but they say such things as, "I tried God's way, and it didn't work." No—you didn't seriously and consistently try God's way, or you would know it does work. In all likelihood the person who gives this excuse is a person who has not sought out the full wisdom of God on a matter or a person who has tried a mixture of his way and God's way. In either case he has refused to obey God completely. If this is your reasoning, I encourage you to go back to God's Word and read every passage that relates to your concern or issue. Then, do what God's Word says!

Or they may say, "I don't think God is concerned about that area of my life." Yes—He is. God is concerned about every aspect of your life, matters large and small.

Second-guessers might say, "The Bible was written thousands of years ago—times have changed." Technology has changed, but the human heart hasn't changed. The Bible is as applicable today to matters of human behavior as it has ever been.

Healthy human beings don't do things that they strongly believe will cause them harm, pain, or irretrievable loss. For a person willfully to choose a way other than God's way, that person must believe that he knows better what will bring him joy, happiness, and gain. If you are in disobedience to God, ask yourself why. On what do you base your decision—even your subconscious decision—that you know more than God knows, or that your choices are better for your life than His choices?

Ultimately, you must trust God that what He tells you is best for your life. You are likely to face times when it seems to you on the basis of your past learning or experience that God's way is not applicable to your circumstance. In those times, you need to move counter to your natural instincts and totally embrace by faith what God says, trusting that your loving heavenly Father is leading you along a path that will eventually bring you joy and fulfillment.

Consider the situation of a man who faces two job offers that seem equal in their challenge and opportunity. One of the offers brings with it a significant increase in salary, but it means moving away from the city, school, and church where he and his family are involved and where they are experiencing spiritual growth and blessing.

In his heart, the man has a prompting of the Holy Spirit to accept the lower-paying position in order to remain in his home, community, and church. Everybody around him, however, encourages him to take the bigger salary. What should he do? Without a doubt . . . obey the prompting of the Holy Spirit! I would encourage that man to trust God to provide additional income or promotions right where he is. God will honor his monetary sacrifice to bring blessing to his family.

Faith is required in every important decision or choice you face. You aren't going to know the full outcome of any major decision in advance of making it. We all are put into the position of obeying God and trusting Him with the consequences of our obedience.

Other second-guessers say, "God's way doesn't always make sense to me." God's ways don't always appear to make sense to any person! It didn't make any sense for Gideon to reduce his armies from thousands to three hundred. It didn't make any sense for Joshua to send the Israelites marching silently around the walled city of Jericho as a battle strategy. It didn't make any sense for David to go after the champion warrior of the Philistines armed only with a slingshot and a handful of stones.

What God calls us to do may not make sense to us. We may be able to come up with all sorts of excuses for not obeying. In the end, however, there's only one wise choice: Obey God.

A DILIGENT COMMITMENT
TO SEEK GOD'S WISDOM

One of the main admonitions for acquiring wisdom is that we seek it. This requires a commitment on our part—it requires diligence that is unwavering. God's Word says,

> My son, if you receive my words,
> And treasure my commands within you,
> So that you incline your ear to wisdom,
> And apply your heart to understanding;
> Yes, if you cry out for discernment,
> And lift up your voice for understanding,
> If you seek her as silver,
> And search for her as for hidden treasures;
> Then you will understand the fear of the LORD,
> And find the knowledge of God.
> For the LORD gives wisdom;
> From His mouth come knowledge and understanding;
> He stores up sound wisdom for the upright;
> He is a shield to those who walk uprightly. (Prov. 2:1–7)

The pursuit of wisdom is clearly an active process. It involves inclining one's ear, applying one's heart, crying out or lifting up one's voice. It involves seeking and searching. Read Proverbs 2:4 again: "If you seek her as silver, and search for her as for hidden treasures."

I can guarantee you that if I announced from the pulpit one Sunday that I knew with certainty that any person who would travel one hour north of Atlanta on a certain highway, turn onto a specific dirt road, travel four and one-half miles, turn onto another dirt road and travel one hundred yards, park under a giant tree to the right of the road, and then dig down four feet would find a million dollars' worth of old silver coins . . . the church auditorium would empty quickly! People would be eager to get their tools together, fill up the car with gasoline, and head out to search for such a tremendous treasure.

God says that wisdom is more valuable than any amount of tangible treasure. Are you willing to make the effort to search for wisdom?

ESSENTIAL #2: PRAY FOR WISDOM

A second essential for acquiring wisdom is to ask God for wisdom. Our proper position before Him is to request wisdom with an attitude of humility and faith.

HUMILITY

Wisdom is imparted only to those who are willing to bow their hearts before the Lord and say, "Not my will, but Yours." Proverbs 11:2 tells us, "When pride comes, then comes shame; but with the humble is wisdom."

Those who remain proud and unyielding before the Lord—choosing to do their own thing in life rather than obey God's commands—will experience shame. They will suffer from their own errors and sins. They will experience the negative consequences of their own greed, bitterness, anger, fear, frustration, doubt, and hatred—and the consequences they experience will be evident to others around them. There is no such thing as private shame—the negative consequences experienced by the proud always come to light and are observed by other people.

Those who are humble acknowledge that they have weaknesses . . . that they don't know everything . . . that they need direction or guidance. Our prayers should reflect our hunger for God, our yearning for Him, our need for Him, and our desire to grow in our relationship with Him.

FAITH

Our prayers must not only be clothed in humility, but also filled with faith. The Scriptures tell us:

> If any of you lacks wisdom, let him ask of God, who gives to all liberally and without reproach, and it will be given to him. But let him ask in faith, with no doubting, for he who doubts is like a wave of the sea driven and tossed by the wind. For let not that man suppose that he will receive anything from the Lord; he is a double-minded man, unstable in all his ways. (James 1:5–8)

Wisdom is not imparted to those who are tossed about in their spirits by unbelief or doubts. Wisdom is imparted only to those who trust God with their lives and who consider themselves to be totally reliant and dependent upon God. It is to those who know that they are nothing without God, but also know that they can do all things with God's help, to whom God will impart His wisdom.

What causes our faith to waver? First and foremost, our own sin. No person who is willfully rebelling against God can ask God for wisdom with a firm expectation of receiving wisdom. His own guilt gets in the way—it clouds his faith. You cannot have strong faith and live in sin simultaneously.

Another cause for wavering faith is a doubt about God's love, mercy, or forgiveness. No person who questions God's motives or mercy will ask God for anything with strong faith. His feelings of self-disapproval and self-condemnation get in the way.

If you want wisdom, pray for it with humility and faith.

ESSENTIAL #3: MEDITATE ON GOD'S WORD

How many times have you found yourself saying at the end of a day, "When I got up this morning, I certainly didn't think I was going to have to face that today"? Our daily lives tend to be a mixture of negative and positive surprises. Rarely can we anticipate all that will happen to us.

We need to have a fresh encounter with God's Word as we prepare ourselves to walk into each new day. And then, all through a day, we need to turn our minds back to what we have read not only in the morning, but also in days past.

Joshua found himself at an interesting point in his life one morning. Moses had died, and Joshua had been among those who mourned his death for thirty days. Joshua had been Moses' top administrator all the years the Israelites had wandered in the wilderness—he had served as Moses' personal assistant as well as the commander of the Israelite army. But God had never told Joshua the full extent of His plan for his personal life.

Then the morning came when God said to Joshua, "Arise, go over this Jordan, you and all this people, to the land which I am giving to them—the children of Israel. Every place that the sole of your foot will tread upon I have given you" (Josh. 1:2–3).

What an awesome challenge! Talk about a life-altering day and an unexpected word from God.

The Lord then gave this promise to Joshua, "No man shall be able to stand before you all the days of your life; as I was with Moses, so I will be with you. I will not leave you nor forsake you" (Josh. 1:5).

Along with God's awesome command came God's awesome words of comfort and assurance. God said to Joshua, in essence, "Here's your part." He said,

> Only be strong and very courageous, that you may observe to do according to all the law which Moses My servant commanded you; do not turn from it to the right hand or to the left, that you may prosper wherever you go. This Book of the Law shall not depart from your mouth, but you shall meditate in it day and night, that you may observe to do according to all that is written in it. For then you will make your way prosperous, and then you will have good success. (Josh. 1:7–8)

Joshua was commanded to meditate on the law day and night—continually. He was to talk about the law—to recite aloud the law to his own heart and mind, and to make certain that all he said to others was in full accordance with the truth of God's Word. He was to do the law—to apply God's principles to his life without wavering, compromise, or hesitation. He was to meditate on God's law to the point that his automatic instinct would be to do what the law said.

To meditate on God's Word requires first that we read it. You can't think all day about something you haven't read!

To meditate means to dig into the deeper meaning of what God is saying in His Word. We aren't just to skim the Bible's pages, limit ourselves to our favorite verses or passages, or read at the surface level. We are to read the whole of God's Word so we can avail ourselves of the whole of God's truth. We are to read slowly, intently, looking for new insights. We are to dig for the deeper meaning of God's Word by asking questions such as:

- What caution is God giving me?

- How does this passage challenge me? What is God calling me to do . . . to change . . . to heal?

- What encouragement is God giving me in this passage?

- As I read this passage, in what ways do I feel convicted by the Holy Spirit to repent of sin or amend error?

You may say, "But I don't always understand the Bible." The best way to begin to understand the Bible is to read more of it. Start with the four Gospels—Matthew, Mark, Luke, and John.

Focus on the words of Jesus. You'll understand enough of what Jesus says to bring about changes in your life. And the more you read, the more you will understand.

Not understanding all you read is no excuse for failing to read your Bible. Rather, it should be the very reason you commit yourself to reading the Bible more frequently and studying it more deeply.

Anytime we face an issue that we know is truly important, we need to go to the Word of God to find out what God says on the matter. God has not left out any topic—He has left no void regarding those things that are most important in life. The Bible is God's viewpoint; it is His opinion, His counsel, and His advice.

We only need to look at our own lives, or the lives of others close to us, to recognize that the vast majority of problems and troubles that we human beings experience are the result of our not following God's commandments. Either we have not known God's commandments or principles, and therefore have not kept them, or we have willfully violated God's commandments. Either way, we suffer the consequences for not keeping God's commands.

Suppose you go to work tomorrow morning and the moment you walk in, one of your colleagues rips into you. He unleashes anger and frustration at you in a way that almost feels like an assault. From your viewpoint, there is no cause for this verbal attack—it's nine o'clock in the morning and you haven't even poured yourself a cup of coffee, much less had a chance to converse with this person. How do you respond?

The world's normal response would be for you to say to yourself, *Hmm—that was uncalled for. I'm going to get back at that person.* The normal fleshly response would be retaliation of some kind. And the godly response? "Is there anything else you want to tell me? I appreciate your letting me know how you feel. I'll consider what you've said" (Luke 6:29 and Rom. 12:19).

One way leads to an argument, division, confusion, unrest, and an escalation of anger, bitterness, frustration, and estrangement. The other way—God's way—leads to peace, understanding, resolution, reconciliation, and potential growth in a relationship.

God's commandments, statutes, precepts, and principles cover all of life's situations. We need to ponder God's Word—read it, study it, memorize it, think about it, and consider it. In doing so, we discover the wise way to handle life and to respond to the difficult situations we all face.

RESULTS FROM MEDITATING ON GOD'S WORD

Here is what happens to us as we meditate on God's Word:

> Oh, how I love Your law!
> It is my meditation all the day.
> You, through Your commandments, make me wiser
>   than my enemies;
> For they are ever with me.
> I have more understanding than all my teachers,
> For Your testimonies are my meditation.

I understand more than the ancients,
Because I keep Your precepts.
I have restrained my feet from every evil way,
That I may keep Your word.
I have not departed from Your judgments,
    For You Yourself have taught me.
How sweet are Your words to my taste,
Sweeter than honey to my mouth!
Through Your precepts I get understanding;
Therefore I hate every false way.
Your word is a lamp to my feet
And a light to my path. (Ps. 119:97–105)

Let me call your attention to important principles in this passage:

The first principle is "A Grid of Truth." Notice that God's Word has made David wiser than his enemies, his teachers, and the "ancients" in his court—the elderly scribes and sages of his day. David may not have known more facts than those around him, but he knew more truth. God's Word is the wisdom of wisdom, the truth of truth, and David had steeped himself in God's truth "all the day."

Each of us has a mental grid—all that we have been taught has been placed on that grid, and this grid functions as a filter for evaluating new information. All new information is processed according to what we have been taught in the past and the perspective, opinions, and attitudes we have developed.

Some of us have faulty grids. We have been taught incorrectly in the past. Anytime you find something in the Word of God that doesn't match your mental grid, it is time to change your grid. The Bible is our sourcebook for truth. It holds out to us the mental grid we all should have been taught.

Our mental grid is strongly influenced by repetition. The more we hear information, the more frequently we encounter concepts, the more deeply that input is etched into our minds. That's why it is so important to read the Bible daily and repeatedly. We learn through repetition.

We can learn something about this from television commercial makers. Commercials are placed at high points in dramatic stories on television so a viewer is primed for new input. And then, those commercials are repeated and repeated . . . day in and day out, week in and week out. The commercials are also couched in terms of sensory experience—the taste, the smell, the feel, the sound, and the exhilaration. We begin to want what we see advertised because we want to feel and experience what the people in the commercials seem to feel and experience.

In like manner, we need to prime our minds for receiving the truth of God's Word—going to the Bible with a heart that is open and a mind that is looking for personal application. We need to be fully alert, fully focused, and ready to hear from God as we read.

We also need to read the stories of the Bible in Technicolor, imagining how the people in the stories felt as they heard Jesus teach His parables or how those who experienced Jesus' miracles experienced a change in their lives. And we need to ask at all times, "What would I have felt? How would I have responded? Jesus is the same yesterday, today, and forever, so how is it that

Jesus wants to deal with me today?" We need to personalize and to apply the Bible to our lives, and not only once but repeatedly, day in and day out. We need to search out ways in which God's Word changes our way of thinking, responding, and believing so that our hearts and minds more clearly reflect God's heart and mind.

Allow the Word of God to persuade you. Allow the Word of God to influence your thinking. Allow the Word of God to alert your perspective and change your behavior.

No matter what any human being may say to us, if any part of that message does not line up with the Word of God, it needs to be dismissed. The Word of God is the standard by which all instruction should be evaluated.

Another important principle we can learn from this passage is "Right from Wrong." Notice that David said his repeated and constant meditation on the Word of God is what kept him from evil and taught him right from wrong. David grew to hate every false way. He knew what was wrong, and he rejected what was wrong.

One last principle we can learn from the passage is "A Lamp to His Faith." Notice that because David knew God's Word thoroughly and was quick to respond to it, the Word had become a lamp to his feet, a light to his path. God's Word clearly revealed to him the way in which he should walk—or in other words, the decisions and choices he should make at any given time. God's Word showed him which alternative to take, which option to pursue, which strategy to employ. He knew when, how, and where to apply God's Word in times of trouble.

Now isn't that what we all want? Don't we all want to know the wise choice, the wise decision, and the wise method quickly and decisively?

David had many counselors—brilliant and courageous "mighty men" who surrounded him with advice. But David relied first and foremost on God's Word to be his counselor. He turned first to what God had to say anytime he faced bad news or difficult circumstances. He found not only comfort but also joy in what he read and studied—he found confidence that God was with him. We read in Psalm 119:

> Princes also sit and speak against me,
> But Your servant meditates on Your statutes.
> Your testimonies also are my delight
> And my counselors. (vv. 23–24)

Certainly not all choices or decisions are ones that can be made instantly. But we can trust God's wisdom to be revealed to us so that we make wise choices and decisions in a timely and effective manner. We can trust God's wisdom to be imparted to us so that we turn from those things that are false, harmful, or sinful, and turn toward what is right in God's eyes. We can trust God's wisdom to give us direction and guidance on a daily basis—from hour to hour if need be.

REMEMBERING WHAT WE READ

Note what the psalmist had to say about meditating on God's Word:

I will meditate on Your precepts,
And contemplate Your ways.
I will delight in Your statutes;
I will not forget Your word. (Ps. 119:15–16)

King David spent a lot of time reading, studying, and thinking about God's Word. He delighted in his study and reflection on God's principles. He not only committed God's Word to his memory, but he frequently recalled God's Word and steeped his thinking in God's law. He did not forget God's Word when it came time for him to speak, to act, or to compose songs. Rather, what he had been thinking about became his speech, his lyrics, and his motivation for behavior. He reflected God's Word in the judgments he made.

God's Word was "sweet" to David—in fact, he said it was sweeter than honey—because the end result of applying God's Word was pleasant, beneficial, and good. A sweet experience is always one in which we find ourselves being helped or blessed. The application of God's Word resulted in constant rewards for David, which no doubt made David all the more eager to meditate on God's Word and apply its truth to his life!

ESSENTIAL #4: ACTIVELY OBEY AND APPLY GOD'S WORD

To walk wisely, we must actively and diligently obey and apply God's Word to our lives. It's not enough to hear God's Word, to read it, or to meditate on it. We must do it. We must apply God's principles and commandments to our everyday lives. We must infuse our minds and hearts with God's Word so that our resulting words and actions are a display of God's commands in action. Every chore, every meeting, every conversation, every task can be a way of expressing obedience to God's Word.

In Proverbs 2:7 we find this: "He stores up sound wisdom for the upright." God has provided in His Word all that we need, but we are the ones who must choose to walk "upright." To be "upright" is the result of right living; it is the product of obedience. The "upright" isn't a class of people to whom God reveals wisdom—as if we were to say that God reveals His wisdom to those who are tall, short, thin, fat, blond, brunette, and so forth. It is those who choose to obey God and who follow through and do what God commands who become the "upright."

Those who are willing to obey God's Word are going to be the ones who are most clearly and directly impacted by God's Word. They have set their minds and hearts to know God's Word. They read God's Word with the thought: *I've got to see what God wants me to do. I'm going to discover today some of the ways God wants me to live and respond and initiate action. I'm reading my Bible for guidance for my life, not just to have something good to read for my mind.*

Proverbs 2 begins, "My son, if you receive my words [or sayings], and treasure my commands within you" (v. 1). Meditating on God's Word is a two-pronged process: We must read the Scriptures as if every one of them applies to us personally and we must receive the teachings of God's Word into our hearts, souls, and minds. And then, we must value His commandments so much that we do what His Word says to do. In other words, we must know God's commandments, and we must place high priority on keeping them.

God's Word admonishes us:

> My son, do not forget my law,
> But let your heart keep my commands. (Prov. 3:1)

> My son, give attention to my words;
> Incline your ear to my sayings.
> Do not let them depart from your eyes;
> Keep them in the midst of your heart.
> For they are life to those who find them,
> And health to all their flesh.
> Keep your heart with all diligence,
> For out of it spring the issues of life. (Prov. 4:20–23)

> Hear instruction and be wise,
> And do not disdain it. (Prov. 8:33)

"Hear" in this verse literally means "heed." We are to act on instruction. And action is key, as in the following verse: "The wise in heart will receive commands" (Prov. 10:8). To "receive" is active. There is nothing passive about God's commands. They are issued in order that we might do them.

No general in an army issues commands to his troops just to hear the sound of his own voice. He gives commands because he expects his troops to take action, to follow through, to fulfill a mission. The same is true for the Captain of our souls!

I quickly discovered when I went to college that there was a big difference in the way I read my textbooks and the way I read a novel. I read a textbook with the intent that I needed to remember the information because I was likely to be tested on it later. I needed to learn what was there because I was going to have many occasions to apply what I read in the course of my life. The more I saw myself being able to one day apply the information I read, the more interested I was and the more diligent I was in studying the material.

The number one reason to read your Bible is not to say you have read it . . . it isn't even to say you've learned what's in it. The reason to read your Bible is to get your marching orders for the day and for the whole of your life. The reason to read your Bible is to grow in your relationship with the Lord and do what He tells you in His Word to do.

Our growth in understanding is cyclical—we read, we apply, we read again, we apply again, and all along the way, we grow in our understanding. As we grow in our understanding, we also grow in our appreciation of the Scriptures and in our eagerness to read the Bible. When you see that the Bible really works in your life, in the life of your family, and in your relationships at work, in the community, and at church, you are going to want to read your Bible more and apply it in more and more ways.

What About Mistakes in Application?

Will we make mistakes as we attempt to obey and apply God's Word? Of course. We are imperfect people. But it is only in doing God's Word that we learn how to better apply His Word.

When you were a child, someone could have told you how

to walk. You could have heard twenty lectures on the mechanics of walking. But it was only as you attempted to walk—getting up, falling down, getting up again, taking a few steps and then more steps—that you learned to walk. The same is true for God's Word. It is only as we apply it—sometimes failing, sometimes not doing everything perfectly, trying again—that we learn how to live in accordance with God's commands.

When a wise person sees his error, he confesses his error or sin to God, makes a change, and moves forward to correct his error and try again.

The acquisition of wisdom only comes as we live out our obedience. How can we ever truly know that God is faithful if we never trust Him? How can we ever fully know what God will do with our lives if we never step out in faith to trust God to help us do more? How can we ever know the joy of winning souls for the Lord if we never open our mouths to give witness to Jesus Christ?

In like manner . . . how can we become wise if we never apply God's commands to our lives?

You can never know fully what God will do in your life, through your life, or all around your life unless you act on everything that God tells you to do.

ESSENTIAL #5: BE SENSITIVE TO THE PROMPTING OF THE HOLY SPIRIT

The very first prompting of the Holy Spirit that any person experiences is to accept Jesus Christ as one's personal Savior, and then to follow Jesus Christ as the Lord of one's life.

After we have received Jesus as our Savior, the Holy Spirit dwells within us to guide us in the way we should walk—the choices and decisions we should make, the work we should undertake, and the new attitudes and opinions we should adopt. Jesus said that one of the primary roles of the Holy Spirit is to guide us into all truth (John 16:13).

When God wants to clarify the next move He has for us, or to move us in a new direction, He very often creates what I call a "prompting" in a person's spirit. A prompting is like a flash of lightning in a person's spirit that creates an almost immediate knowing of which way to turn, what to do, what to say, how to respond. The prompting comes with a deep assurance and confidence that the choice or decision is right.

Anytime you have a prompting of the Holy Spirit, you can be assured that our all-wise God—the omniscient Holy Spirit—is saying to you, "I love you enough to tell you what to do in this situation."

Much of what the Holy Spirit prompts us to do involves a potential loss or gain of something important or valuable. At times the Holy Spirit prompts us to take an action that could result in a loss or gain in the life of another person.

There are certain things we should avoid . . . should discard . . . should ignore . . . should put away. There are other things that we should reach out and receive . . . should pay attention to . . . or should act upon.

As much as the Holy Spirit prompts us to do or to say certain things, He also prompts us not to act or to speak. There have been times when I have clearly felt the Holy Spirit prompting me, "Sit down and don't say a word." There have been times when I have felt the Holy Spirit telling me to do nothing in a particular situation, even though everything in me was boiling and eager to take action.

How do you develop this sensitivity? Ask God to make you sensitive to the prompting of the Holy Spirit. The work of imparting sensitivity to you is His work. However, if you fail to act on the prompting that the Holy Spirit gives you, you will never learn how to follow the Holy Spirit's leading. When you experience what you believe to be a prompting, act on it immediately. Don't second-guess what God tells you to do.

You will quickly discern if you have heard correctly. If you have not heard correctly, you will feel unrest in your spirit; you will not have peace. On the other hand, if you have heard correctly, you will feel a growing peace and confidence at the action you have taken.

As in most things in life, we learn by trial and error.

A few months ago, I flew home from a pastors' conference I had addressed in another state, and as I stood up to leave my airplane seat, I had a strong prompting of just one word, "Look!"

I glanced around as I prepared to leave the plane, and I didn't notice anything. The truth is, I didn't seriously heed that prompting. After I had walked away from that plane and was about halfway down the concourse, I thought, *I should call to make certain the person who is picking me up is on his way.* I reached for my cellular phone and discovered that it wasn't where I usually keep it. I searched my briefcase and pockets . . . no phone. Suddenly I remembered that I had used the phone on the plane before takeoff, so I concluded it must still be there. I walked back to the gate only to discover that the doors to the aircraft had been locked. It took a few minutes, but I finally found someone who would let me back onto the aircraft. And sure enough, when I searched more diligently, I found my cellular phone tucked into the space between the seat and the armrest. A simple glance hadn't been enough, but that wasn't what the Holy Spirit had prompted. He had said, "Look!"

That was a simple matter, but my failure to heed this prompting wasted a good half hour of my time, and about the same amount of time in the life of the person who was waiting at the curb to pick me up—time in both of our lives that could have been used in more productive ways.

You may be asking, "Does the Holy Spirit really lead us in such practical, simple matters?" Yes, He does. He leads us in matters great and small—nothing is beyond the knowing of the Holy Spirit. The closer we follow Him and the quicker we are to heed His prompting, the more detailed and practical it seems the Holy Spirit functions in our lives.

Let me give you another example that I heard about just recently. A young woman was facing a decision about where to go to college. She and her parents had narrowed the choice to four Christian colleges, and her parents left the final choice to her. They encouraged her to pray and ask the Lord where He wanted her to go.

The first two colleges she visited resulted in a clear "no" from the Holy Spirit. She felt uncomfortable or ill at ease before she had spent two hours on either of the first two campuses.

Although these were good schools with excellent reputations, she knew in her spirit that they were not right for her. It wasn't anything a specific person said or did; she just felt restless in her heart.

The last two colleges, however, seemed almost equal as she weighed them in her mind and heart after visits to the campuses and conversations with others who attended the colleges. She finally decided one evening to attend the college that was closest to her home. She announced to her family that she had made her choice, and she went to bed. She later recounted what happened: "I was awake most of the night. I tossed and turned and felt miserable. I had a nagging feeling that I was making a mistake and that feeling just wouldn't leave me."

The next morning, this young woman announced to her mother, "I think I made the wrong choice. I am changing my decision." She later told her parents and grandparents, "I felt peace all day. By the end of the day, I knew without a shadow of a doubt that I had finally made the right choice." The issue had been settled definitively as far as she was concerned.

As the days and weeks before she left for college unfolded, she came to the point where she said, "I can't imagine ever having had a problem in deciding. My choice seems so right that it's difficult to believe I ever even considered the other three schools." After one semester at the college, she wrote to her parents, "I couldn't be happier. I'm glad I learned to hear God for myself and that I did what He led me to do."

This young woman had experienced a series of promptings that led her to the final decision that was God's best plan for her. Now let me ask you: Do you believe this young woman has a much clearer understanding about how the Holy Spirit speaks in the human heart and prompts a person to move into right actions or decisions? Absolutely. She has learned a tremendous lesson about what it means to hear from God and to walk wisely.

You may be saying, "Well, this sounds like intuition." I encourage you to change your vocabulary. If you are a believer in Christ Jesus, you have the Holy Spirit living inside you, and He desires to lead you step-by-step into the fullness of God's plan and provision for you. Intuition for the believer has a name: Holy Spirit.

WHEN WE FAIL TO HEED GOD'S PROMPTING

What should you do if you fail to heed a prompting of the Holy Spirit? First, confess that you have made a mistake or a sin against God. Receive His forgiveness. But then, take a second step. Ask yourself, "Why did I fail to heed this prompting? Why didn't I act immediately on what I felt the Holy Spirit was telling me to do? How can I keep this from happening again?" Don't just confess your error—learn something from it!

I learned from that incident in my life not to lay my cellular phone down after I've completed a call. Instead, I put it back in its case and in the place I have designated for it in my briefcase or luggage.

Now a cellular phone is a fairly minor thing to almost lose. There are far more important things that we are in danger of losing if we don't heed the Holy Spirit. Not only can we lose possessions, but also we can lose our health, a relationship we deeply value, an opportunity that won't come our way again, or an encounter that could make a significant difference in our lives.

Ask the Holy Spirit to help you heed His promptings in the future. And then . . . heed them!

ESSENTIAL #6: OBSERVE GOD'S WORK

To acquire wisdom, we are challenged by God's Word to "study" God's work in the world around us. God calls us to observe His handiwork in order to learn His ways. Every creature, every natural law, every event, and every human being contains a wide variety of lessons about the methods God uses, the desires of God's heart, and the nature of God's eternal plan. The world around us is a reflection of God's creativity, personality, and unchanging nature.

LEARNING FROM NATURE

We don't need to look very far to see that God has made every creature with a unique form—no two blades of grass or snowflakes are exactly alike, and neither are human beings.

We don't need to look far to see that God has a sense of humor and delight and joy—He has built into virtually all living creatures a desire for peace and a means of expressing joy. Just listen to a kitten purr or watch a puppy wag its tail.

We don't need to look far to see that the laws of nature don't change. Gravity is the same today as it was yesterday. The sun comes up every morning.

In just these few examples, we see wonderful lessons that God's methods are always subject to change. His love for each of us is one-of-a-kind, but His principles do not change. What important lessons these are about the nature of God!

God's Word says in Proverbs 6:6, "Go to the ant, you sluggard! Consider her ways and be wise." You may think, *Well, what can I learn from an ant?* I recently posed that question to a group of people, and they quickly responded:

- Cooperation
- Perseverance
- Diligence in working
- Sacrifice
- Strength in working together
- Unity of purpose

In my opinion, that's a lot to learn from one of the smallest of God's creatures! And if you have ever had ants in your kitchen or been bitten by a large ant, there are still other lessons you might learn!

Jesus said,

> Look at the birds of the air, for they neither sow nor reap nor gather into barns; yet your heavenly Father feeds them. Are you not of more value than they? Which of you by worrying can add one cubit to his stature? So why do you worry about clothing? Consider the lilies of the field,

how they grow: they neither toil nor spin; and yet I say to you that even Solomon in all his glory was not arrayed like one of these. Now if God so clothes the grass of the field, which today is, and tomorrow is thrown into the oven, will He not much more clothe you, O you of little faith? (Matt. 6:26–30)

Jesus did not tell His followers to study the writings of some famous scholar in order to understand God's message—He said simply, "Look around you. Look at the birds and the flowers! The world is filled with lessons about God's provision and faithfulness."

If you want to be wise, pay attention to the world around you. Learn from what you see, hear, and sense.

LEARNING FROM EVENTS

The Lord desires for us to learn not only from the natural world, but also from the events He allows to occur in our lives. For example, when we face a problem or suffer a calamity, we need to say to God, "How do You see this? What purpose do You have in allowing this to happen to me? What lessons are there for me to learn from this experience?"

We might regard something as an awful accident . . . but God doesn't consider anything to be an accident. Nothing occurs by happenstance. God is not out of control at any time. Even if the entire world seems to be in chaos—God is still in charge!

We might regard something as being a shocking surprise . . . but God is never surprised. Nothing catches God off guard.

We might regard something as being a terrible curse . . . but God does not willfully send harm to His people. God comforts and leads us through difficult times and tragedies that result from our living in a fallen world in which the devil is still afoot.

Study events. See the hand of God in them.

LEARNING FROM OTHER PEOPLE

God not only desires that we learn from nature and from events and experiences, but that we become students of human behavior. His Word says, "A wise man fears and departs from evil, but a fool rages and is self-confident" (Prov. 14:16). Haven't you seen evidence of this? Those who are in rebellion against God tend to be angry, arrogant people. On the other hand, those who serve God do not seek out evil environments or associate with evil people—they run from evil.

Study other people. Look at those you consider to be wise. Observe them. What can you learn from them? Look at those you consider to be foolish. What behavior do they exhibit? What can you learn from them?

Look not only at what people have and do. Rather, focus on the outcome of their lives. Take a look at how they respond to tragedies and catastrophes. Study their character. In Proverbs 1:10 we read, "My son, if sinners entice you, do not consent."

The following verses then give examples of how sinners operate. They "lie in wait" and "lurk secretly" to see whom they might rob or destroy. But what happens when calamity strikes? The Bible tells us they have no place to turn:

When your terror comes like a storm,

And your destruction comes like a whirlwind,

When distress and anguish come upon you.

Then they will call on me, but I will not answer;

They will seek me diligently,

    but they will not find me.

Because they hated knowledge

And did not choose the fear of the LORD,

They would have none of my counsel

And despised my every rebuke.

Therefore they shall eat the fruit of their own way,

And be filled to the full with their own fancies.

    (Prov. 1:27–31)

Haven't you seen this with your own eyes? Don't you know people—or know of people—who have openly and defiantly rejected God and have sought to acquire all they can at the expense of others, only to become sad, lonely, bitter old people? They die surrounded by their fancy possessions without any comfort from God or other people.

Learn from people! Learn things to do. Learn things not to do. What happens when a person tithes? What happens when a person doesn't tithe? What happens when a person stops praying or reading the Scriptures? What happens when a person spends time every day in prayer and Bible reading? What happens when a person stops attending church regularly? What happens to those who not only attend regularly but also become actively involved in a church?

What happens when a person drinks alcohol excessively . . . smokes two packs of cigarettes a day . . . uses illegal drugs or abuses medications . . . has illicit sexual affairs . . . squanders his income or resources in gambling? What is likely to be the quality of a person's health and relationships if he doesn't drink, doesn't smoke, doesn't take drugs, doesn't commit adultery, and doesn't squander his resources in frivolous activities, get-rich-quick investments, or gambling?

Be observant. Learn from the examples of others.

ESSENTIAL #7: ASSOCIATE WITH AND LEARN FROM WISE PEOPLE

Build friendships, business associations, ministry partnerships, and other alliances only with people you genuinely be-lieve to be walking in the wisdom of the Lord (2 Cor. 6:14). The Bible is very clear on the benefits that come by associating with wise people: "He who walks with wise men will be wise, but the companion of fools will be destroyed" (Prov. 13:20).

"But how," you may ask, "can I tell if a person is wise?"

Go back and read the seven admonitions I have just given you! The wise person is going to be someone who is seeking wisdom, meditating on God's Word, actively obeying and applying God's Word to his life. The wise person is going to be someone who is observing God's work in the world, praying for wisdom with humility and faith, and being quick to seek out and receive godly counsel from others. The wise person is going to be someone who has wise friends, wise professional colleagues, and wise business associates.

Who influences you the most? To whom do you listen most intently? Whom do you "follow"? Whom do you admire or seek to be like? Whose words mean the most to you? The answers to those questions reveal much about you.

Now ask yourself: "Is the person who influences me the most a genuinely wise person? Does the person I admire the most and seek to be like a person who is actively acquiring more and more of God's wisdom?"

What is the character of your close associates? Is their influence for your eternal good?

Do your friends or close colleagues freely and frequently talk about God or God's Word . . . or are they uncomfortable every time the name of Jesus is introduced into a conversation or the Bible is mentioned?

Do your friends or close colleagues encourage you to make decisions based upon God's commandments and principles . . . or do they dismiss the commandments of God as being unimportant or irrelevant?

Do your friends or close colleagues tell you when they think you are doing something that is wrong in God's eyes . . . or do they entice you to sin?

Do your friends or close colleagues build you up by reminding you of God's love . . . or do they drag you down, criticize you, or make fun of you?

Choose your friends and associates. Don't just accept people into your life solely because they live close to you, you have known them for a long time, or you feel obligated by them to be a friend or colleague. Choose your friends and associates on the basis of their character and commitment to Christ. Choose wise, godly people. They will be a blessing to you. And through the influence of their relationship with you, you will grow in wisdom.

SEEK GODLY COUNSEL

If you find that you need specific counsel, seek out a godly person who is an expert in that area or who has experience in the very circumstances in which you find yourself. Follow the suggestions that are based upon God's Word.

None of us do well in walking through life alone. We need to be in close communication and association with other people who believe in Christ Jesus, are studying God's Word, and are seeking to follow Christ daily.

We need to spend some time with people who have been through experiences that we are facing. We also need to spend time with people who have succeeded in an area of life in which we would also like to succeed. We need to talk things over with them, learn from them, and receive their wise counsel.

Read what the Word of God says about this:

> The way of a fool is right in his own eyes,
> But he who heeds counsel is wise. (Prov. 12:15)
> By pride comes nothing but strife,
> But with the well-advised is wisdom. (Prov. 13:10)

The ear that hears the rebukes of life
Will abide among the wise.
He who disdains instruction despises his own soul,
But he who heeds rebuke gets understanding. (Prov. 15:31)

Listen to counsel and receive instruction,
That you may be wise in your latter days. (Prov. 19:20)

There are times when we need to hear someone say to us, "Don't do that." "You shouldn't do that." "Get rid of that habit."

There are times when we need to hear encouraging counsel from someone: "Do this!" "Take hold of this opportunity." "Apologize to that person." "Reach out to that person."

Thousands of therapists' offices are filled with people who come to hear what a counselor has to say to them, and then they go home and promptly forget all they've heard. They do not truly listen to what the counselor says and then put it into practice.

I recently talked to a person who had gone late one Saturday night to visit a woman who was seriously distraught that she had lost custody of her only daughter and was now being openly rejected by that daughter every time she tried to exercise her visitation rights. This mother could not be consoled or comforted. She could not be counseled. She refused to believe that God still loved her, that God could bring about a change in the heart of her daughter and in their relationship, or that God still desired to bring about something good in her own life.

If you flat-out reject the wise counsel or the godly encouragement of others and refuse to heed the Word of the Lord they share with you, you very likely are going to fall victim to oppression and depression.

Seek advice from godly experts. If you need financial advice . . . go to someone who is skilled in the management of money. If you need advice related to contracts . . . go to a skilled and experienced lawyer. If you need advice about your health . . . go to someone who specializes in the area that pertains to your health-care concern. And if you need advice about relationships, spiritual matters, or your personal development . . . by all means go to a Christian therapist, counselor, or psychologist.

Seek out a counselor who believes in God's Word and who personally seeks to follow Christ Jesus. Seek out a counselor who desires the best for your life but who will speak the honest truth to you. Seek out a person whose lifestyle is godly. Seek out a person who will give you advice that is based upon scriptural principles. If you have any doubt about the counsel you are receiving, ask the person, "Do you believe in Jesus Christ as your personal Savior? Do you believe the Bible is God's truth for how we are to live?"

Good counseling always includes a balance of admonition, reproof, discipline, approval, and encouragement. If a counselor only addresses the negative all the time, run from that person. If a counselor only agrees with you or applauds you at all times, run from that person as well. Neither person is going to help you consistently over time because progress toward health and wholeness requires that we make changes, turning from bad habits and embracing good habits in our thinking and behaving.

Change, in turn, comes only after we honestly appraise both what is wrong in our lives and what is good in our lives.

Are you willing to be convicted? Are you willing to receive the appreciation of others? Are you willing to open up yourself to change?

All godly counsel is ultimately encouraging, even if it initially involves reproof or correction. Listen closely if someone appears to be critical of your actions or attitude. If you know that person loves you, take the counsel to heart. Weigh what he says against the Word of God. Ask others who will be honest with you if the reproof you have received is valid. Ask the Lord to reveal to you the error of your ways. Don't reject criticism out of hand. What you perceive initially to be negative criticism may actually be positive criticism that can lead to your growth and more success in life.

It is pride that keeps us from seeking or accepting godly counsel. Face up to that fact. If you truly want all the benefits of wisdom, you must humble yourself and seek out help from others.

TAKE COURAGE!

Read again what God said to Joshua: "Only be strong and very courageous." God wants us to be wise, but it takes strength and courage to pursue, acquire, and apply wisdom.

I went to a meeting one night scared all the way down to my toes. I didn't want to attend that meeting. I was fearful about what might happen at that meeting. But I was also certain of one thing: God wanted me there. I could not walk out of that meeting because I knew to do so would be to disobey God. And if I had disobeyed God at that point in my life . . . would God have blessed my future ministry? No. I would not be experiencing all that I experience in ministry today if I had disobeyed God at that important juncture of my life. Fear, yes. Obedience, always.

A number of years ago as I was preparing to move to Atlanta, I was praying one day, and God showed me in a momentary vision a large, dark cloud hovering over the city skyline. I knew trouble was awaiting me in Atlanta. That knowing did not give me joy. I don't enjoy conflict any more than the next person. Yet conflict is exactly what erupted several months after I moved to Atlanta. Fear, yes. Obedience, always.

God does not promise us a life without storms or thorns. He does promise us His presence, His help, and His rewards for our obedience in doing what He calls us to do.

At times our first response to God's leading in our lives is fear. We find ourselves saying, "Oh, God, surely You wouldn't call me to do that? Surely I must have heard You incorrectly." However, the more we argue with God or try to ignore His leading, something inside us grows and churns and causes us to know, "This really is what God wants." At that point of knowing, we face the decision to obey or disobey. Obedience, especially when a situation seems risky, takes courage.

God challenges us repeatedly throughout our lives. From His perspective, we never "arrive" at any point in our lifetimes. There is no retirement from God's development process, no plateau on which He calls us to rest for the remainder of our lives. God continually calls us to take steps that are just one degree beyond our current ability. God continually seeks for us to grow in our faith, develop in our ability to minister, and mature spiritually. He continually moves us out of our comfort zone into a courage zone.

Change of any type—including positive growth—requires courage. But the good news is this . . . God only requires you to have the courage to take the next step. He doesn't ask you to have the courage for the full race before you start running it.

Consider the situation of a young man who feels called to preach. If that young man looks at the long run of his future, he is likely to get discouraged. He might find himself quaking in fear as he asks, "Where am I going to get enough material to preach sermons every Sunday morning for the next forty years—not to mention sermons for Sunday night or Wednesday night or special revival services?"

That question can't be answered. That young man needs to trust God to give him a sermon for next Sunday. Believe me, after forty years of preaching, I'm still trusting God for just one more sermon—the one I have to preach next Sunday.

So often people refuse to do the will of God because they fear failure. Let me encourage you—God does not set us up for failure. He does not call us into a situation in order to watch us fall flat on our faces.

Moses may have thought God was calling him to fail. From a human perspective, it isn't wise for a person who has run from legal prosecution to return to the leader of the land with a stick in his hand and declare, "Let God's people go." Moses had all sorts of arguments for God—"I'm nobody," "I don't know what to say," "I can't talk very well." He expressed his fear that nobody would believe him or listen to him. He pleaded with God to send someone else (Ex. 3–4).

In the end, however, Moses obeyed. He took one step at a time—he met his brother, Aaron, whom God had prepared to help Moses. He met with the children of Israel. He met with Pharaoh—again and again, through ten plagues that followed Pharaoh's refusal to allow the Israelites to leave. Moses took one step at a time out of Egypt and across the wilderness and up Mount Sinai to meet with God.

At no time did God reveal to Moses all that he would face in his obedience, but at all times God said to Moses, "I am with you. I am leading you to the place I have prepared for you and for My people."

That same promise of God is ours. God promises to be with us always. He promises to lead us to the place He has prepared for us. Our part is to trust Him step-by-step.

❊

FIVE

WISDOM FOR
CONFRONTING TEMPTATION

I must admit—a head of lettuce has never called to me from my refrigerator late at night. A pint of good-quality chocolate, strawberry, butter pecan, or peach ice cream, however . . . that's another story. I am sometimes amazed at how quickly ice cream can disappear from my freezer.

All of us face temptations—no believer is ever immune to them. Some of the things that tempt us seem to appear on a daily basis.

What is the strongest temptation you face regularly? Do you find that you yield to this temptation more often than you resist? What is it about that particular temptation that motivates you to give in, even though you know the Word of God commands otherwise?

All of us have areas of vulnerability and times when we are less strong. Have you ever identified the areas of your life or the times in which you seem especially vulnerable to temptation?

All of us are responsible for our own behavior and choices. We cannot avoid temptation, but we can control our response to temptation. If we yield to a temptation, we can choose our next response. Is your first reaction after you have yielded to a temptation to blame God, someone else, or a circumstance?

THE NATURE OF TEMPTATION

Temptation is an enticement of our natural, God-given desires to take them beyond God-given limits or boundaries. Let's take the desire to eat as an example. There's nothing wrong with eating—we all need to eat. Hunger is a natural, God-given impulse. But there are also God-given limits for how much we are to eat and what we are to eat to remain healthy. As another example . . . there's nothing wrong with sexual behavior within the God-given limitation of marriage. When we go outside the boundary of marriage, we move into the zone of sin.

THE SOURCES OF TEMPTATION

Temptations are from three main sources: the world, the flesh, and the devil.

The World. We all face countless temptations heaped on us by the world at large. The visual media present to us an onslaught of images of things we surely must want in order to be acceptable, powerful, or attractive. The enticement is held out to us continually to buy more, enjoy more, feel more, and have more. You define more of what—more power, more sex, more fame, more pleasure, more money, more applause, more, more, more.

The Flesh. We face the temptations that arise from our own senses and our physical and emotional needs. Our basic natural drives as human beings are those drives related to our needs for food, shelter, warmth, affection, sex, companionship, acceptance, worthiness, and purpose.

The Devil. We face temptations directly from the devil. He entices us in the same way he tempted Jesus—to believe that we are above God's laws when it comes to our self-gratification, to seek to be worshiped and adored by other people, and to manipulate and to rule over others for our own gain (Matt. 4:1–11). The devil has been tempting mankind from the very beginning. He hasn't changed either his purpose or his methods.

DOES GOD TEMPT US?

What about God? Does He tempt us? No. The Bible is very clear on this point:

> Let no one say when he is tempted, "I am tempted by God"; for God cannot be tempted by evil, nor does He Himself tempt anyone. But each one is tempted when he is drawn away by his own desires and enticed. Then, when desire has conceived, it gives birth to sin; and sin, when it is full-grown, brings forth death. (James 1:13–15)

God will never entice a person to act in a way that is contrary to His commandments. He does not have any association with sin, and He certainly does not entice His people to sin and suffer sin's consequences.

People have said to me from time to time, "I've prayed and prayed, but God hasn't removed this temptation. I don't know why He continues to tempt me." These people have confused temptation—which is an enticement to disobey God's commandments—with times of trial or testing, which are always allowed by God so that we might become stronger, purer, and more mature in our faith and more effective in our witness. God tests us so we might remove sin from our lives or manifest His faithfulness to us. He tests us so we might grow and develop in ways that bring God's approval and authorization for ministry. Times of trial are for our good.

In sharp contrast, temptations come with the purpose of defeating us, trapping us, enslaving us, and ultimately destroying us. God allows us to be tempted—it is part of His gift of free will to us—but God never initiates temptations, and He never gives us permission to yield to them.

An Act of Rebellion. Our yielding to temptation is ultimately an act of personal pride and rebellion against God's commandments. When we yield to temptation, we are saying to God, "I want what I want rather than what You want. I want my needs met in my way, in my timing, for my own self-satisfaction."

When we yield to temptation, we feel guilt and shame. Our relationship with God becomes estranged. We feel less worthy and less accepted by God—we feel of less value.

The end result of temptation is our enslavement to sin. The devil's lie to us is that one drink won't hurt us, one affair won't destroy us, one angry outburst won't damage a relationship, or one more helping won't kill us. The temptation always begins as a fine thread . . . that becomes a string . . . that becomes a rope . . . that becomes a noose.

Is temptation a sin? No. It is not a sin to be tempted. Jesus was tempted and the Bible clearly states that He lived His life without sin or deceit (1 Peter 2:22). Sin occurs when we yield to temptation. It is at the point where we give in to a temptation that we sin.

A thought popping into your mind is not a sin. Jesus had to think about what the devil said to Him in the wilderness; He had to deal with the tempting thoughts that the devil prompted. The thought of sin is not at all the same as an act of sin. It is when we act on tempting thoughts in a way that crosses the boundaries of God's commands that we enter into sin.

If Satan whispers to you, "Well, you've been thinking about it . . . you might as well do it," your response should immediately be, "Oh no. Thinking and doing are dramatically different things!"

DEALING WITH TEMPTATION WISELY

To deal with temptation wisely, we must understand several things about the nature of temptation. The apostle Paul wrote to the Corinthians:

> Let him who thinks he stands take heed lest he fall. No
> temptation has overtaken you except such as is common

to man; but God is faithful, who will not allow you to be tempted beyond what you are able, but with the temptation will also make the way of escape, that you may be able to bear it. (1 Cor. 10:12–13)

These two verses are packed with truth.

ALL ARE TEMPTED

Nobody is above temptation. The moment you think you are too strong to be tempted, too righteous to be tempted, or too spiritually mature to be tempted . . . you are setting yourself up for a fall.

Even Jesus was tempted. Three times during a forty-day stay in the wilderness, the devil came to the Son of God and tempted Him to misuse and then to abandon His relationship with God the Father. If the devil had the audacity to tempt the only begotten Son of God, and with such high stakes, what makes you think you are ever above and beyond his temptations?

Now, there are some forms of temptation that are not likely to impact certain people. Not every person can be tempted by everything, and not all people are tempted by the same things. Each one has a propensity toward a certain temptation. Temptations also may change as a person moves through the various stages of life. What tempts a person when he is a teenager may not be what tempts him when he is fifty years old.

Not only are we all subject to temptation, but we must recognize that we never become an expert in handling temptation. No person ever reaches a point in his life where he can afford to be careless with fire. A child certainly can't afford to be careless with matches . . . but neither can an adult. Fire has devastating potential, and it always must be handled with caution. The same is true for temptation.

Any person who drives a car, and especially on our freeways, knows that you can never allow yourself to become careless as you drive. The same goes for any pilot: No matter how experienced he or she may be, the pilot knows that every squall or storm front holds the potential for disaster. No matter how experienced a driver or pilot may be, conditions always require that he drive or fly with extreme alertness and caution. The wise person lives in this same state: alert and cautious. We should always be ready to withstand temptation. The devil does not give up.

There never comes a time when we should arrogantly assume, "I can handle this. I've withstood this temptation so many times that I'm immune to the effects of this temptation." When you let down your guard and are careless in the way you deal with a temptation, you are setting yourself up for disaster.

People have said to me through the years, "I don't believe a mature, godly person is tempted as much as an unbeliever." My response is this: A mature, godly person is probably tempted more than an unbeliever is! The unbeliever is already in the devil's camp—why does the devil need to waste his time tempting him? The mature, godly believer is the person who is likely to inflict the most damage on the devil's enterprises. Isn't the most dangerous enemy the one a person is most eager to destroy?

A person is either an enemy or a friend of the devil. Those who are enemies of the devil are likely to be the main targets of his temptations.

Years ago, a man cautioned me, "If you ever take the InTouch ministry overseas, watch out. It's one thing to broadcast the gospel where the name of Jesus is still revered by a significant percentage of the population. It's an entirely different story when you broadcast the gospel in areas where the influence of the devil is strong and the name of Jesus is hated with a vengeance." This man was exactly right.

The moment we made plans to launch out into a worldwide daily broadcast of the gospel, the devil did his utmost to attack us from every angle possible. Our response? Keep praising God, keep obeying God, and keep broadcasting!

TEMPTATIONS ARE UNIVERSAL

All forms of temptation are universal. There isn't anything you will face that hasn't been experienced by countless other people, both now and throughout history. Technology has advanced through the years, but human nature has not changed. We err greatly if we ever conclude, "This temptation is peculiar to me. I'm being tempted in a way that is unique—it's a stronger temptation or a more enticing temptation than others feel. Nobody else can understand what I'm going through. I doubt if any person would ever be able to resist this temptation; surely God doesn't expect me to resist it."

Every one of those conclusions is a lie.

OUR HELPER IN RESISTING TEMPTATION

The Holy Spirit helps us to resist temptation—regardless of the nature of the temptation. This isn't true for those who have not received Jesus Christ as their Savior and have been given the Holy Spirit to indwell them as an ever-present Counselor, Comforter, and Source of power. The unbeliever is on his own when it comes to temptation. The believer, in contrast, has One who helps him resist every form of temptation. The believer has the assurance that God will not allow him to be tempted beyond what he is able to handle as he relies on the Holy Spirit for help.

We must own up to the fact that we do not "fall" into a temptation idly or casually. We walk into temptation, and sometimes we run into it. A yielding to temptation is not something that just happens to us. The will is involved. There is always a moment when we can say no. It is at that moment that we must turn to the Holy Spirit and say, "Help me!"

What is your first response when you face temptation? Do you begin immediately to rationalize the situation because you know you are going to yield to the temptation? Or do you immediately go into "resist mode," relying on the Holy Spirit to get you through the moment?

GOD ALWAYS PROVIDES A WAY OF ESCAPE

God promises to provide a way of escape for every form of temptation so we are able to bear it. God never promises to remove temptation from our lives. Rather, He gives us the power to resist temptation, endure temptation, and overcome temptation.

The response of many people to temptation is to attempt to run from it. But to where and to whom are you going to run? You won't escape temptation by running to another job in another city. You won't escape temptation by running to a new church or a new neighborhood. You won't escape temptation by running to a new relationship. The famous line from children's literature is true for people of all ages: "No matter where you go, there you are!"

Certainly there are times we need to flee. Paul wrote to Timothy, "Flee also youthful lusts" (2 Tim. 2:22). There are times when you need to get up and walk away from the table, move away from the person who has cornered you, or get out of the situation, room, or conversation. But a life pattern of fleeing isn't going to resolve the issue of temptation. There comes a point where we need to stand up to a temptation and say no to it. We can't outrun a propensity to give in to a particular sin. We need to face that area of vulnerability in our lives and deal with it.

But how? How can we defend ourselves against temptation?

BUILDING A DEFENSE AGAINST TEMPTATION

For us to build a good defense against temptation, we must put several control mechanisms into our lives, all of which work together.

1. Resolve to Obey God. If you have never fully settled the issue of obedience in your life, make a commitment today to choose obedience to God's commandments. Say to the Lord, "I choose to obey You. I know I will be tempted, but I choose to do things Your way. I choose to rely on You to help me live a godly life."

Establish in your heart a desire to resist evil and stand against temptation. Having this resolve in place prior to facing a temptation can make a tremendous difference in whether you cave in to a temptation or successfully resist it.

Then, take your commitment a step farther. Visualize yourself saying "no" to a temptation that you believe is likely to strike your life. Visualize yourself being offered an alcoholic drink at a party . . . and then see yourself saying "no" to that drink and accepting instead a cup of tea or a soft drink. Visualize yourself standing in a store staring at an item that you'd like to own but know you shouldn't purchase . . . and then visualize yourself saying "no" to that purchase and walking out of the store. As you visualize yourself resisting temptation, say to yourself what God's Word says, "In Christ, I can do all things. God's strength is sufficient for me. I am a new creation in Christ Jesus, and my mind is being renewed by the power of His Holy Spirit. God has not made me for sin but for righteousness, blessing, and victorious living. Thank You, Lord, that You are adequate. You are helping me in all things, in all ways, at all times." Speak God's Word into your heart.

This form of visualization of godly behavior combined with verbalization of God's Word and your faith in God is a potent form of mental rehearsal. When we practice godly behaviors and responses in our minds and hearts, we are far more likely to demonstrate those behaviors and responses when temptations come our way.

Don't play the same old failure tapes in your mind. Create new tapes! Visualize yourself walking in purity and strength. Verbalize your faith and trust in God.

2. Identify Your Personal Areas of Frequent Temptation. Some areas of your life may involve nearly constant temptation. These are the areas of your vulnerability and the areas in which you need to confront temptation directly.

There are people who are so fragmented emotionally that they find themselves yielding to temptation without virtually any thought whatsoever. They simply go with the flow of their immediate impulses. If that is the case with you, you need to address your emotional health and get help.

3. Address the Needs That Make You Vulnerable. Address the neediness of your own life. A temptation always strikes at an area of need we perceive—it may be a need for higher self-value, attention, appreciation, or approval; a need for love and affection; a need that is physical or sexual; or a need rooted in loneliness or pride, among others. Ask yourself immediately in the face of temptation, "Is there another way—a good way, a right way—of getting this need met in my life?" The answer is always "yes." God always has a godly alternative for meeting the deep needs of your life. He wants you to have His wisdom about how to meet your deepest emotional needs. Search God's Word. Get godly counsel. Face up to your neediness and identify God's solution, God's answer, and God's methods.

4. Short-Circuit the Thought Process of Temptation. We need to understand the process of temptation in order to understand how better to short-circuit the process.

All temptation begins with thoughts, usually ones that seem to pop into our minds out of the blue. One of the prime times for these thoughts to occur is during prayer. If you tell me that you have never had a sudden, wicked thought while you are praying . . . I'm going to question the amount of time and the intensity with which you pray! One of the choice times for the devil to attack us is when we are talking to God. It's then that the devil often brings up our past and our present to "accuse" us before the Lord.

We have a choice when temptation hits our minds—we can hold on to that idea. We can harbor it, nurture it, feed it, entertain it, and allow it to grow. Or we can quickly shut it out and force ourselves to think about something else that is virtuous.

If we choose to hold on to a tempting idea, it will turn into a fantasy. In the stage of fantasy, we find pleasure in thinking about something that is contrary to God's wisdom. We mold the idea into one that tickles our fancies, delights our senses, and brings us a good feeling. We imagine what it would be like to own a certain object, partake of a certain substance, or enter into a relationship with a certain person, and always with an overtone of pleasure and self-gratification. We enjoy the fantasy.

If we do not put a stop to the temptation at this stage, the fantasy will grow into a desire. We begin to actually imagine fantasy turning into a reality. We begin to desire the thing or experience we have fantasized.

A desire calls the will into the equation. We face a choice about whether to act on it or not. If we consent and make the choice to act on the illicit desire, we sin.

The sequence for every temptation we face is thought, fantasy, desire, choice, and willful decision to yield. The process may happen very quickly—in a matter of seconds at times. At times we may be so deep in the habit of yielding that thought and decision seem to happen almost simultaneously.

The farther we go in the process of temptation, the more difficult it is to resist. The faster the process from thought to consent, the more likely we will consent, and the more likely this area of temptation has been faced repeatedly in the past and has become a habit in our lives.

Some time ago, I had a conversation with a young woman who had been through a divorce. The man she married had fallen into deep sexual sin. I asked her when she thought the problem had begun. She said, "Probably in his childhood. I know when he was a teenager, he and his friends regularly looked at pornographic magazines."

Then she said, "The problem probably was triggered, however, on our honeymoon. We went to San Francisco, and on the second day of our marriage, he went out to jog through the city and was gone for nearly two hours. Looking back, my suspicion is that he jogged through a part of town where sexually explicit photos and sex shops and homosexual meeting places abound. Since he was gone so long, I suspect he not only jogged past those photos, but also probably went into some of those shops and bars. Things were never right after that day. I truly believe the things he allowed to enter and lodge into his mind on that morning were seeds that later became a harvest of sexual sin."

The best time to put a stop to any temptation is when it is still an idea. We need to confront temptation to sin with an idea that is godly. That godly idea may be a prayer for God's help . . . a refocusing of the mind on a goal that the Lord has set before us . . . or a verse of Scripture that we repeat to ourselves aloud.

If you have identified a specific area of vulnerability in your life, begin to arm yourself now with Scriptures that address that area of weakness. Memorize verses to recite in the face of temptation. Prepare yourself in advance so that when the white-hot moment of temptation comes, you will have a full scriptural arsenal as part of your response.

5. *Confront the Element of Deception.* The promise of sin is immediate satisfaction without penalty. The truth is that there is always a penalty to sin. That penalty may not be as immediate as the satisfaction, but it will come. This is especially true of sexual sin. Sexual sin is not only extremely harmful to a person, but it is a sin that easily becomes habitual. Every act of sexual sin weakens a person's ability to withstand future temptations to engage in sexual sin. A person who has one affair is far more likely to engage in a second affair, and then a third, and so forth. Those who are highly promiscuous have virtually no ability to say "no" to sexual temptation.

You may be thinking, *I see people all the time who are promiscuous, and they suffer no penalty for their sin.* You may not be able to see the penalty, but it's there, already at work eating away at their emotional and physical health and already doing its destructive work in their spirits. Even if the person claims to feel no guilt, it's there. Even if the person does not feel that he has fragmented his emotions, he has.

One of the most severe penalties for repeated sexual sin manifests itself when a person finally meets someone he comes to love deeply and to whom he desires to commit himself fully. He faces an inability to give himself fully to the one he loves.

If that is the case in your life, you must face your sin and ask God to forgive you, to cleanse you, to heal you, and to restore to you an ability to be faithful to one person for the rest of your life. Ask God to give you the ability to love generously and wholeheartedly.

A defense mechanism we can develop against temptation is to steep ourselves in the truth of God's commandments and promises. We need to have a clear understanding of the inevitable and eventual consequences of sin. If you know a stove is hot, you are less likely to touch it. If you know a bush has long, sharp thorns, you are less likely to push your way through it. An awareness of sin's penalty acts in the same way. It serves as an invisible barrier to help keep us from crossing the line from desire to consent. If you don't stay in the truth, you'll stray into a lie.

Ask yourself immediately in the face of temptation, "Is this idea in keeping with God's Word? Is this temptation a violation of God's commandments? What are the consequences if I yield to this temptation?" Evaluate both the immediate and the long-range consequences. Evaluate the consequences to others around you. Evaluate the impact on your future life and effectiveness in God's kingdom.

Ask yourself, "Am I prepared to pay the consequences? Am I prepared to lose far more than I will ever gain?"

At times, of course, we are not able to see situations with clarity. We may have trouble discerning if something is a temptation. We may have difficulty keeping ourselves focused on the big picture of our lives.

For those reasons it is very important that we put ourselves into a relationship with a person who will hold us accountable for our behavior.

6. *Put on the Whole Armor of God.* Another very valuable defense you can build into your life is one that I personally have used for many years. Countless people to whom I have taught this defensive tactic have told me how valuable it is in their lives. I strongly recommend it to you: Every morning, before you get out of bed, put on the whole armor of God. Paul wrote in Ephesians 6:

> Finally, my brethren, be strong in the Lord and in the power of His might. Put on the whole armor of God, that you may be able to stand against the wiles of the devil. For we do not wrestle against flesh and blood, but against principalities, against powers, against the rulers of the darkness of this age, against spiritual hosts of wickedness in the heavenly places. Therefore take up the whole armor of God, that you may be able to withstand in the evil day, and having done all, to stand.
>
> Stand therefore, having girded your waist with truth, having put on the breastplate of righteousness, and having

shod your feet with the preparation of the gospel of peace; above all, taking the shield of faith with which you will be able to quench all the fiery darts of the wicked one. And take the helmet of salvation, and the sword of the Spirit, which is the word of God; praying always with all prayer and supplication in the Spirit, being watchful to this end with all perseverance and supplication for all the saints. (vv. 10–18)

What does it mean to put on this armor every day? It means praying, "Lord, I put on the helmet of salvation to protect what I think. I put on the breastplate of righteousness to protect my emotions. I gird my loins with truth so I might produce and create in truth, not error. I put on the sandals of the preparation of the gospel of peace so I might be a messenger of God's love and mercy. I pick up the sword of the Spirit so the Word of God might work in me and through me today. I carry the total-body shield of faith to protect me against all the temptations, accusations, and assaults of the devil against my life, my mind, and my heart." Putting on the armor of God is putting on the strength of Jesus Christ. It is declaring that He is our Lord and we are His servants.

This discipline of putting on the whole armor of God every morning is a powerful reminder to our own spirits that we do not live for ourselves, but we live and move and have our being in Christ Jesus. It is a powerful reminder that we must rely upon the Holy Spirit to guard what we think, how we feel, where we go, what we produce, what we believe, and how we respond to life.

7. *Maintain a Big-Picture Focus.* The devil's lie to us at all times

is to focus on what we want. Part of his temptation to us involves a shutting out of what God's Word says, what other people think, what the law says, what common sense dictates, and so forth. He brackets out anything that might act as a restraint.

If I am out in the snowcapped mountains on a photography trip, I have a number of options. I can use a wide-angle lens to try to take in the full panorama of a mountain ridge. Or I can put a longer lens on my camera and focus on one aspect of a mountain—a particular ravine or glacier or outcropping of rock. If I put on an extremely long lens, I may be able to focus on the behavior of a single mountain goat or bear. Once I am looking through a strong telephoto lens, I no longer have a sense of the big picture of the mountain scene. I have zeroed in on only one element, and that element dominates my concentration.

The same happens in a temptation to sin. When we focus only on what we need in a given moment, we lose all sense of the big picture of our lives. We shut out all thoughts of penalty for sin, and we focus only on the pleasure we believe we will experience. In order to build a defense against this tactic of the devil, we need to keep the big picture of our lives always before us. We need to stay in the Word of God on a daily basis. We need to read the Bible every morning and then intentionally recall what we read periodically throughout the day. We need to have our radios tuned to Christian stations that give us godly messages and Christ-honoring music. We need to spend time with family members and friends to keep our perspective on life more fully rounded—we need to maintain a sense of obligation, responsibility, and duty to those we love.

8. Guard the Gates of Perception. We also need to guard what we take into our lives. The best place to put a stop to food temptations is at the grocery store, not when you are staring into your well-stocked pantry or refrigerator. Simply don't bring home the foods that are tempting to you. If I don't have peach ice cream in the freezer, I can't be tempted to eat a bowl of it before bedtime. In like manner, the best move to take in counteracting a temptation to overspend or to purchase frivolous items on impulse is to stay out of the mall and turn off the television set. Refuse to watch the shopping channel. Refuse to spend time idly floating through a shopping center just to see what's available. If you find yourself tempted to watch certain programs or movies that you know do not depict godly behavior, refuse to sign up with your cable or satellite dish provider for the stations that carry those programs.

Don't go to the places where you routinely find yourself tempted. Don't hang around the people who routinely try to talk you into behavior that you know is sinful. Don't purchase an item to "try," knowing in advance that the substance has the potential for harm.

Anticipate trouble points—go over your day's agenda with the Lord early each morning and specifically ask for the Holy Spirit's help and guidance as you enter situations or encounters that you believe may produce temptation.

Guard yourself against putting yourself in a personal circumstance in which your perception may be clouded. A word I recommend frequently is HALT:

H = Hunger. Never allow yourself to become too hungry.

A = Anger. Never allow yourself to become too angry.

L = Lonely. Never allow yourself to become too lonely.

T = Tired. Never allow yourself to become too tired.

It is when we are hungry, angry, lonely, and tired that we are most prone to yield to temptation. It's easiest to overeat or eat the wrong foods when we are famished. It's easiest to reach out to someone who is wrong for us when we are extremely lonely. It's easiest to use substances to calm us down when we are seething with anger. It's easiest to be talked into sinful behavior when we are tired physically.

Also recognize that some occasions during a year may be a prime time for temptation to strike. The occasion may be an anniversary, a holiday, a birthday, or some other time of general celebration. Those are occasions when we feel more like indulging ourselves, either as a personal reward or as compensation for hurtful memories associated with that event in the past.

9. Build Accountability into Your Life. Accountability is especially important if you find yourself facing temptations frequently, or if you find yourself dealing with the same temptation repeatedly. Find a loyal, devoted, Christ-serving, Bible-believing mentor, counselor, or close friend who will call you to account for your behavior. Admit the areas of temptation that seem especially strong in your life. If a temptation strikes and you are struggling to resist it, call this person. Admit the feelings you are having and ask for the person's encouragement, advice, or prayer. Ask this person to check up on you periodically and to question how you are handling your propensity to sin in a particular area of your life.

Many groups designed to help people with addictions have sponsors to whom an addict can turn for support, encouragement, and counsel. This is actually a biblical principle. Jesus sent out His disciples to do their work "two by two." Part of the reason was for mutual support and encouragement; part of the reason was for mutual accountability, wise counsel, and prayer. The truth of God is established out of the mouths of two witnesses—when you are routinely speaking God's truth to yourself, and a close friend is also routinely speaking God's truth to you, God's truth is going to dominate your thinking and behaving.

You must want to be able to resist temptation and to be made strong in areas where you are vulnerable. You must choose obedience.

10. Cry Out to God for Help. Remember always that God is in control at all times—He does not abandon you in temptation situations or say to you, "You're on your own in this matter." No! He is with you at all times and in all situations, and He desires for you to ask Him for help any and every time you are tempted.

Furthermore, God has put limits on the degree to which we are tempted. He is the One who will help you escape the snare of temptation. Your ultimate defense in times of temptation is to cry out to God for His help.

If you have yielded to temptation, or if a particular temptation has become a habit, you especially must call out to God.

Only God can deliver you from the bondage you have put yourself in.

I recently heard the story of a man whose beloved wife had died from a suffering, painful disease when she was only in her forties. This man had served God all his life, but in the aftermath of his wife's death, he became very angry with God for not healing his wife. He began to avoid going to church, associating with strong Christians, reading his Bible, and praying. Instead, he began spending his time with an ungodly woman who was flashy, daring, and energetic—all of which signaled life to him in the face of his grief and sorrow. In spite of the counsel of his children, his brothers and sisters, his parents, and many of his strong Christian friends, he moved in with this woman. He lived in a hellish state for nearly six years. Their relationship was marked by nearly constant argument, thrown vases, abusive language, alcohol use, and a total avoidance of godly events, friendships, or disciplines.

Then the day came when this man called out to God. He said, "I knew I was at the end of myself. I had no ability in myself to say 'no' to this woman or to say or do the things I knew were right. I cried out to God, 'Please forgive me. Help me!' Almost immediately, I had the courage to move out of this relationship and to refuse all contact with this woman. I also had the courage to crawl humbly back to my family and friends and ask for their forgiveness and help."

If you are stuck in the consequences of temptation today, cry out to God for His forgiveness and assistance. He will hear you and answer you in His mercy.

STAND STEADFAST

As you stand against the onslaughts of temptation, verbalize frequently your faith in God's ability to help you withstand temptation. Voice your faith in His presence with you, your dependency on His strength, and your belief in His promise to help you.

I have absolutely no doubt that if you will put these ten safeguards against temptation into your life, God will honor your efforts and help you withstand temptation.

SIX

WISDOM IN CHOOSING FRIENDS AND BUSINESS ASSOCIATES

W hen you identify your assets in life, what do you list? Many people think of assets in terms of real estate, stocks and bonds, or material possessions. Some think in terms of natural talents or spiritual gifts.

The dearest treasure of your life—second only to your relationship with Jesus Christ—is a close friend.

A friend loves you unconditionally, catches you when you fall, believes in the best for you and encourages the best in you, shares your deepest concerns, applauds your successes and feels your pain, offers you constructive criticism in times of error, and feels sorrow for you in times of pain or rejection. A genuine friend is a gift of God's mercy to you.

God's foremost wisdom regarding our friendships and business associations is this: Be careful whom you choose. Never assume that just because a person seeks you out, you are in close proximity to a person, or an acquaintanceship with a person seems to develop quickly that God has sent this person to you. Ask Him!

Parents often have to say to their children or teenagers, "I want you to have good friends, but I am concerned about one or two of your friends." Although a child may protest, parents have the authority and responsibility to keep a child from forming friendships that they believe will be harmful to their child's spiritual or emotional development and, in some cases, their physical safety.

What is your criterion for choosing a person to be your friend? Are you drawn to appearance, possessions, fame, or power? Ask yourself what appeals to you—and then quickly ask yourself if this is a godly character trait.

Where do you go to find friends? From time to time when I go out to eat, I take a moment to glance into the bar or lounge adjacent to the restaurant. Usually I am in a restaurant about the time of the so-called happy hour, and I want to see if the people in the bar are happy. I have yet to see a happy person in a bar at happy hour. Instead, I see looks of loneliness and some-times despair on the faces of those who are there. As far as I'm concerned, it's never wise to start a friendship solely on the basis of loneliness, and certainly not if the person is dousing his loneliness with a chemical substance. Such a relationship has a strong likelihood of ending in pain, disillusionment, and disap-pointment.

If a friendship is ever based on a personal need, it likely will develop in a warped way.

Do you choose Christians to be your friends? Too often, I

hear people say, "I know my friend isn't a Christian, but he's a good person," or a teenager will say, "I know this person I'm dating doesn't go to church and hasn't accepted Christ, but I want to date this person anyway."

Anytime you put a qualifier of "but" on a relationship with an unbeliever, you are headed for a fall. God warns us: "Do not be deceived: 'Bad company corrupts good morals'" (1 Cor. 15:33 NASB).

"But my friend has good morals," you may say. That's not the main principle involved in this verse. The truth is, those who are not Christians influence the behavior and character of Christians far more than Christians influence the behavior and character of unbelievers.

Don't enter into a friendship or relationship hoping or believing that you will win that person to Christ and then everything will be perfect. You may witness to that person, but in the end, you are not the one who brings a person to salvation—that is the role of the Holy Spirit. You may also influence the behavior of another person, but in all likelihood, the unyielding unbeliever is not going to adopt lasting godly behavior in his or her life—the unbeliever does not truly have the capacity for change. It is the Holy Spirit in us who imparts to us the ability to repent and change the way we think, feel, and respond to life.

Rather than your having influence over the unbeliever, the probability is that the unbeliever is going to convince you to go places or to do things that you would never go or do on your own initiative. The temptations are going to be strong: "You don't know what you're missing" . . . "you could go and influence the people there for good" . . . "you should try this before you dismiss it is as being bad" . . . "everybody does this—don't be a prude."

There is a difference between your developing a relationship with a person in order for you to witness to him about Christ, and your development of a friendship with an unbeliever. If you are trying to win a person to Christ, then your relationship has a very specific goal and purpose. A friendship, however, is for mutual benefit and for the sharing of a common life. A friendship involves a sharing of time, resources, and help. Be cautious in the amount of your time, the extent of your resources, and the nature of the help you give to or receive from an unbeliever.

You must ask yourself, "To what extent am I willing to go to win this person to Christ?" If you do not answer that question up front, you may find yourself sucked into a relationship that is far more pervasive, invasive, and expensive—not only in terms of financial expense but in terms of emotional pain—than you had intended.

From God's perspective, bad company includes anything and any person that draws you away or diminishes the importance of your relationship to Christ Jesus and your following His commandments explicitly. We are never called to compromise character or to have close fellowship with unbelievers. Make certain that the friends you choose share your values, beliefs, and ethical standards.

PEOPLE WHO SHOULD *NOT* BE YOUR FRIENDS

God's Word gives some very explicit advice about who should not become your friend.

AVOID THE PERSON WHO IS A GOSSIP

Many people I encounter, including many Christians, seem to dismiss gossip as amusing, as interesting, and as something that doesn't cause serious harm. God's Word takes a very different approach. In fact, the apostle Paul identified the "busybody in other people's matters" in a list that includes "murderer," "thief," and "evildoer." Gossip murders a person's reputation; it robs a person of the right of innocence until proven guilty, and it judges and condemns a person without a fair trial. God's Word plainly says:

> He who goes about as a talebearer reveals secrets;
> Therefore do not associate with one who flatters with his
>   lips. (Prov. 20:19)

If a person slanders or gossips about other people to you . . . you can be assured that person will slander and gossip about you to others. A gossip does not merely give information in a neutral way or provide facts that can result in help for a person. Rather, a gossip tells tales—partial truths, incomplete facts, slanted stories—for a perverse or self-centered reason, generally to win your favor and to bring some form of detriment to a person he considers to be a rival or a threat. The moment the gossiping person perceives you as a rival or a threat, you can be assured that you will become the subject of tales to others.

AVOID THE PERSON WHO IS QUICK-TEMPERED

Some people seem to be perpetually angry. Their anger may stem from bitterness that began to develop in their childhood because they felt cheated out of something or rejected by a person who was important to them. The root of their anger may be a prejudice or hatred that took root in their lives as the result of pain or sorrow they felt was inflicted on them without cause. Seething, long-lasting anger can erupt without notice.

Other people have grown up in homes where one or both parents exhibited a hot temper. As children, they never learned to express deeply held emotions or convictions without blowing their stack.

The trouble with vented anger is that it damages other people, regardless of the motivation for the anger or the quickness of its rising and fading. Expressions of raw, unmediated, unmeasured, unfettered anger always lead to pain, and usually that pain is felt most intensely by those who are the most innocent.

When you make friends with an angry person, you are going to find yourself developing an angry spirit. What angers him is likely to anger you. The way he expresses anger is likely to become the way you express anger. God's Word is very clear:

> Make no friendship with an angry man,
> And with a furious man do not go,
> Lest you learn his ways
> And set a snare for your soul. (Prov. 22:24–25)

Anger truly is a snare—it keeps us from seeing good in others, it keeps us from quickly and freely forgiving, and it keeps us from expressing the godly character traits of patience, mercy, kindness, and self-control.

AVOID THE PERSON WHO IS REBELLIOUS

Rebellion is not only an angry lashing-out against someone or something—it can also be a quiet, willful resistance that manifests itself as disloyalty or discontentment against those in authority. The rebellious person does not choose to obey—rather, he is pulled in various directions by his own desires and lusts. He is unstable, subject to frequent changes of his own opinion. A rebel reacts to life, sometimes in highly volatile ways. He is not committed to the Lord, nor is he likely to be committed to those in leadership.

The person who is loyal only to himself cannot be loyal to a friend. Avoid friendship with such a person—he can turn on you very quickly and become your enemy. God warns:

> My son, fear the LORD and the king;
> Do not associate with those given to change;
> For their calamity will rise suddenly,
> And who knows the ruin those two can bring? (Prov. 24:21–22)

Avoid the Person Who Is Self-Indulgent

The person who is self-indulgent is not in control of his own desires. His self-indulgence may be manifested as gluttony (consistent overindulgence in food and drink), immoral behavior (an uncontrolled drive to satisfy sexual desires), or greed (an insatiable desire for more and more possessions). The self-indulgent person may be power-hungry or very manipulative because he is always seeking what he wants, when he wants it, without regard to the needs and concerns of others.

If you form a friendship with such a person, you are likely to find yourself being used by that person. He or she will attempt to consume your time, your resources, your energy, and if possible, the time, resources, and energy of those you know. And when he has taken all you have to give, he will move on to the next person. God's Word warns: "Whoever keeps the law is a discerning son, but a companion of gluttons shames his father" (Prov. 28:7).

Have you ever gone to lunch with a plan that you are not going to have dessert or overindulge in carbohydrates, only to find yourself with a person who wants to try everything on the menu from an appetizer to a rich dessert? The other person, of course, wants you to try a bite of everything and won't take "no thank you" for an answer. And in the end, you walk away from that lunch more than full and having completely blown your intention to have a light, nutritious meal.

The fact is, self-indulgent people influence us. They seem to embrace life fully and are always curious and eager to try new things that capture their imagination or tickle their senses. The self-indulgent person can appear to be bigger than life, a lot of fun to be around. But beware! In the end, that person can cause you to throw away your own disciplines and get off track with God's best plan for your life—all in the name of experiencing more of life or having a good time.

AVOID THE PERSON WHO IS SEXUALLY IMMORAL

We live in an age when people are prone to say, "What they do behind closed doors is their business." The truth of God's Word is that we are to judge morality—not judge a person, but judge behavior. We are to know what is right and wrong when it comes to morals and ethics, and clearly so when it comes to sexual immorality. God's Word says clearly:

> A perverse man sows strife,
> And a whisperer separates the best of friends.
> (Prov. 16:28)

> Whoever loves wisdom makes his father rejoice,
> But a companion of harlots wastes his wealth.
> (Prov. 29:3)

"Wealth" in this second verse refers to a person's total substance—one's physical, mental, and emotional health and energy, material resources, integrity, reputation, relationships, and Christian witness. When we engage in sexual immorality, we lose much of who we are as well as what we have.

The Bible is very clear on the issue of sexual immorality. Christians are not to engage in premarital sex (called fornication in some versions of the Bible) or extramarital sex (otherwise known as infidelity or adultery). There are no exceptions. Sexual intimacy is reserved for marriage.

This stance runs one hundred and eighty degrees counter to our culture. Popular music and television programs, even those in prime time that are aired to children, are filled with sexual innuendo and at times, explicit sexual behavior. Movies—even those labeled PG or PG-13—tell our children and teens more about sexual behavior than any sex-education course. From billboards to magazine advertising, sex is used to sell products. The result is an ongoing plague of sexual diseases and unwanted pregnancies, which in turn has led to abortions and unplanned children. When will we wake up?

Even if there was not a strong sexual overtone to much of what we see and hear in a given day, we would still have to face our own physical senses and drives. The Bible tells us that the lust of the flesh tempts us to turn away from God's path of purity and righteousness.

Each of us is moving in one direction or the other at any given time—either we are moving toward fulfillment of our fleshly desires without regard to God's wisdom, or we are moving toward God's way, plan, and purpose. And which direction is easier? The easy way is always the way of the flesh. It is our natural tendency to want to meet the needs and drives we feel—it takes discipline and trust in God not to give in to fleshly desires. An immoral friend doesn't have to talk very long or very hard. The temptation is already there. What we need are friends who help us say "no" to self-gratifying impulses.

You may be saying, "Just because my friend is immoral doesn't mean that I will become immoral."

Perhaps not immediately . . . but if you stay in that friendship, I am strongly convinced that before very long, you will begin to compromise your own moral standards. The compromise may be subtle at first—it may be a change in the way you dress, the vocabulary you start to use, or the things you think or daydream about. The compromise will likely include the jokes you tell and the things you converse about with your immoral friend. Eventually the compromise will lead to a change in the materials you read and see, the way you walk and act around others, and the places you go. Before long, your own sexual desires will drive your life. Rather than have a passion for following Christ, you will have a passion to satisfy your own flesh.

Don't start down that slippery slope. Don't form a friendship with a person you know is immoral.

AVOID THE PERSON WHO IS A FOOL

We tend to think of fools as being silly or frivolous people. The Bible takes a much more serious approach: A fool is a person who has arrogantly chosen his own way over God's way. He has pushed God out of his life. He has refused all discretion, discernment, or wisdom that God's Word offers. Fools are described in the book of Proverbs as being deceitful and slanderous (Prov. 10:18). They laugh at sin (Prov. 14:9). A fool regards wisdom as being too lofty (Prov. 1:7)—a fool shuns wisdom and pursues his own folly.

A wise son makes a father glad,
But a foolish man despises his mother.
Folly is joy to him who is destitute of discernment,
But a man of understanding walks uprightly.
(Prov. 15:20–21)

Those who love the world do not love God. A person who has turned his heart away from the Lord is not going to build up your faith, help you live a righteous life, or encourage you to pursue wisdom. Choose friends who love God and who desire to follow God's commandments!

The Impact of a Good Friendship on Your Life

What is the potential impact of friendship on your life? The potential is one for abundant good.

A Friendship Can Delight You

A good friend will bring joy and pleasure to you. You should enjoy being with or going places with a friend. A wise, godly friend causes you to feel acceptance and love. He or she reflects God's love and care for you. A good friend gives you a feeling of assurance and comfort that you are not alone in this world— someone knows you, understands you, and appreciates you.

A Friendship Can Develop You

A good friend should help you to develop as a person. It is in close friendship that we learn better how to communicate with other people, how to empathize with and help those in need, how to rejoice with those who are succeeding in life, and how to give and take. We learn how to relate on a deeper, more intimate level—we learn how to be more vulnerable and to share who we really are.

A good friend gives a person the freedom to share anything he or she wants to share, without fear of condemnation, judgment, or a pulling away. A good friend will motivate you to grow spiritually. As you open up your heart to a friend and admit your struggles, and as you pray with your friend and discuss the Word of God, your desire for the Lord is increased.

A woman once told me about a few of the temptations she had experienced as a teenager growing up in Florida in the 1970s. She said, "What got me through that time was that I had two good Christian friends. One of them went to my high school and both of them went to my church. The three of us became loyal, true friends to one another and we did a lot of things together after school and on weekends. When one of us felt temptation, we knew we had two friends who would stand with us and help us say 'no.'" She concluded, "You can be strong in the face of just about anything if you have a friend standing on your right and on your left."

A FRIENDSHIP CAN "DRIVE" YOU TO EXCELLENCE

A good friend can be highly motivating. A good friend builds us up so that we want to become and to accomplish all that our friend believes we can be and do.

A good friend accepts the fact that you are imperfect and, at the same time, does his best to help you become more like Christ Jesus. A good friend will not express shock or dismay at your struggles in life, but rather, will say, "We all go through tough times. I'm here for you. I'm going to walk through this with you, pray for you, and you're going to emerge from this stronger."

A good friend can help you become more productive, have a higher energy level, and have more enthusiasm for life. A good friend gives you the confidence to take godly risks, embrace new challenges, and move to the next level in your work or hobby. When you know that someone loves you and is standing with you and believes in you . . . you are far more willing to step out in faith and develop your full potential physically, mentally, emotionally, and spiritually. A good friendship gives you an abiding confidence.

History bears out the truth that most highly successful men have a woman in their lives who loves them, motivates them, encourages them, and helps them to achieve their best and highest. It may be a mother, a sister, an aunt, or a wife. Every good marriage I have ever witnessed bears this quality that both the husband and the wife encourage each other to walk in godly wisdom and to be and do their very best.

THE POTENTIAL FOR NEGATIVE IMPACT

There are also some potential negative aspects to a friendship. Because friendships are valuable and influential, they can hurt us as much as bless us.

A FRIENDSHIP CAN DISILLUSION YOU

A friendship can disappoint you. Without warning, a friend can turn away or disappear. I once had what I considered to be a close friendship with a person who suddenly, and without any explanation, withdrew from our friendship. To this day, I do not know why this happened. He never offered an explanation. I was disappointed to lose this man's friendship.

One thing I learned from that experience was that we must never allow a disappointment in friendship to cause us to become bitter or to close ourselves off from other people. We must never say, "Because that friend hurt me, I'm not going to trust anybody to be my friend in the future."

A FRIENDSHIP CAN DISTRESS YOU

At times, our friends can cause us to feel distress or deep concern. If we see our friend making a choice that we know is unwise, or if we see our friend walking away from Christ, we are naturally going to feel distress. When we truly love others, we find their willful rebellion very troubling.

A FRIENDSHIP CAN DRAG YOU DOWN

Not only can a friendship drag us down into sinful behavior, but a friend can drag us down emotionally. At times a friend can place such high emotional demands on us, or be in such an unhealthy emotional state, that we find ourselves feeling inadequate, fearful, depressed, or angry right along with that person. If a friendship causes you to lose your joy in the Lord, or to feel perpetually angry, bitter, discouraged, or frustrated . . . reevaluate that friendship.

If a friendship is dragging you down, reflect upon your own upbringing and background. Are you repeating negative patterns from your childhood in your adult friendships? Are you emotionally too dependent upon your friend, or have you allowed a friend to become too emotionally dependent upon you? Are you suffering from emotional or even physical abuse from a friend because you learned that pattern of behavior in your early years? Is it easy for you to fall into a mutual pattern of anger, bitterness, or depression in a friendship because you have held these feelings inside you for a number of years?

The health of your friendships is very often directly related to the health of your family during your growing-up years. If your childhood family life was marred by poor communication, power struggles between your parents or siblings, eruptions of anger, fear in a parent, or a withholding of affection . . . you likely will be prone to develop friendships that begin to exhibit the same qualities. Or you may find that friendships become a source of frustration to you because you are seeking a "perfect" friendship that is opposite the home life you had as a child.

There are no perfect friendships because there are no perfect people. There are, however, mature, godly, mutually rewarding and satisfying friendships—and those friendships tend to be ones in which both parties are seeking to become mature, godly, wise people.

A FRIENDSHIP CAN DESTROY YOU

In the extreme, an unwise friendship can so influence you to participate in evil that you experience destruction to your body, your emotional health, your career, or your relationships with family members, other friends, or fellow church members. An unwise friendship can draw you away from Christ and away from all things that are beneficial to you. In the end, an unwise friendship can bring about the destruction of your life.

FRIENDSHIPS CHANGE US

What impact are your friends having on you? Are your friends building you up, bringing you blessing, and drawing you closer to Christ? Are they a genuine delight to you, a help to you, an encouragement to you? Are you a better person because of the friends you have?

Or are your friendships marked by disappointment, disillusionment, or damaging emotions? Are your friends leading you to engage in behaviors that are ungodly? Are they encouraging you to adopt opinions or to hold beliefs that are contrary to God's Word? Are you becoming less joyful, less productive, or less godly as the result of a friendship?

These questions, of course, are valid to ask about a romantic relationship or a professional relationship related to our work or career.

The unalterable fact is this . . . friendships have an impact on our lives—for better or worse. Friendships cause us to grow, develop positively, and change our habits for the better . . . or they stunt our growth, cause us to develop bad habits, and to change in negative ways.

If only for that supreme fact, we need to choose our friends and business associates with care and prayer, always keeping in mind the hallmarks of what a true and godly friend should be. I like this definition that I came across recently:

> A friend should be radical.
> He should love you when you're unlovable,
> Hug you when you're unhuggable,
> And bear with you when you're unbearable.
>
> A friend should be fanatical.
> He should cheer you when the whole world boos,
> Dance when you get good news,
> And cry when you cry, too.
>
> But most of all, a friend should be mathematical.
> He should multiply the joy, divide the sorrow,
> Subtract the past, and add to tomorrow,
> Calculate the need deep in your heart,
> And always be bigger than the sum of all their parts.

Do you have a radical, fanatical, mathematical friend? Are you that kind of a friend to others?

SEVEN

❖

Wisdom for Building Deep, Lasting, Godly Friendships

S everal years ago I had a life-changing encounter with two
men who attend my church in Atlanta. These two men
and their wives were friends for thirty-five years. The two
couples ate together at least once a week, and they frequently took vacations together. They stood by each other as
friends through good times and bad as they raised their children and went through various changes and challenges of
life. And then, within three months, both of the wives of
these men died.

Tragedy had struck in a way that neither of these men had
ever anticipated.

I saw these men in the church one day, and I asked them how
they were doing. They told me about an upcoming trip they
were planning . . . just the two of them. They were about to
head out on a car trip that would take them from Atlanta to
Alaska and back. They were excited about the trip ahead, which

they had mapped out and planned in detail. As I watched them walk away, one word came to mind: *buddies.*

I asked myself, "Do I have a friend like that?" Seeing these two men and the way they had supported each other emotionally, loved each other as brothers in Christ, and encouraged each other gave me a burning desire to have a friend with whom I could share life for thirty-five years. I began to ask myself, "What kind of friend am I? Who are my closest friends? What do I expect from a friendship?" And most important, I began to question, "What does God's Word say about friendship? How are we to build wise friendships that are deep, lasting, and godly?"

GOD DESIRES FOR YOU TO HAVE CLOSE FRIENDS

God desires for you to have close, intimate friendships. There are a number of examples of such friendships in His Word.

Moses had Aaron and Joshua as his close friends. David had a close friend in Jonathan. Daniel had close friends named Shadrach, Meshach, and Abed-Nego. Jesus chose twelve disciples as His friends, and among those twelve, He had a special bond with Peter, James, and John. The apostle Paul had a number of close friends and associates—Luke, Timothy, Mark, Barnabas, and others.

Close friends are a tremendous blessing. We need to cherish and value them.

A LIMITED CIRCLE

How many loving, devoted, loyal, genuinely true friendships do you have? I'm not talking about casual relationships. I'm talking about tried-and-true, long-term, devoted friendships.

Most people could not count five such friendships.

The reasons that people don't have numerous deep friendships seem to be threefold. First, we don't take the time to build such friendships. Second, it's difficult to find friends to whom you can entrust the whole of your life—secrets, dreams, goals, desires, likes and dislikes, accomplishments, pain and hurts, needs, disappointments, and failures. And third, many of us have not learned how to build a good friendship and to resolve the differences of opinion that may occur along the way.

Casual friendships may seem to just happen. True, long-lasting, deep friendships, however, are built. They are established on a commonality of purpose and values; they are built through shared experiences and conversations marked by vulnerability and transparency.

Deep friendship is at the core of companionship, marriage, and mentoring or business partnerships. It is in the context of mutual friendship that we can evaluate many relationships.

From the very outset of human creation, God determined that we human beings have a need for one another. God said about Adam, "It is not good that man should be alone; I will make him a helper comparable to him" (Gen. 2:18). When the Bible uses the term "man," the term generally can be translated "mankind." Even in this very specific incident in which God forms Eve to be the helper for Adam, we can look beyond the immediate situation and see that God was speaking a truth that related to the whole of mankind. People need people. We each need relationships with others who are "comparable to us"—like us in values, desires, goals, beliefs, and to a degree, personality—so that we might receive help from them and help them in return. We need other people in order to grow into the fullness of our own potential and in order that we might experience a mutual giving and receiving of love and kindness.

When God said, "It is not good that man should be alone," that was the first time God had said about anything in His creation, "It is not good." Up to that time, everything God made, He regarded as being totally and wonderfully good. Ask any lonely person today and he or she will confirm to you that loneliness is not good. Ask any therapist or counselor and he will confirm to you that people who live in isolation from other people are not healthy people emotionally or spiritually, and very often, they lose their physical health as well.

Many people read the story of Adam and Eve solely as the story of the first married couple. The creation of Eve was about far more than God providing a sexual companion for Adam. Eve shared the totality of Adam's life. She was a helper "comparable to him" and he, in turn, was of help to her (Gen. 2:20). They shared not only a garden home, but also a purpose for living and a responsibility before God.

God's Word tells us: "A man of many friends comes to ruin, but there is a friend who sticks closer than a brother" (Prov. 18:24 NASB).

This verse may appear to be in contradiction to what I have just said about the value of good friendships. Let me explain what this verse means.

We might read Proverbs 18:24 this way: "A person with

many casual, shallow friendships has nowhere to turn for strength in times of trouble." Casual, shallow friendships crumble in a crisis. People you thought were your friends tend to disappear in times of persecution, criticism, or trouble. "Ruin" in this verse means to be shaken so badly that you fall to pieces. Casual friends do nothing to help you keep yourself together emotionally and spiritually in times of severe loss, rejection, or sickness. Casual friendships have no bonds of strength or tenacity.

In contrast God's Word describes the nature of a close, intimate friend. A real friend is one who sticks closer than a brother—he will be there through thick and thin, in good times and bad. He will provide strength so that you do not crumble in the face of evil or calamity. He remains rock-solid and steadfast in times of trauma.

I am very grateful that I have a handful of genuine friends who stick by me no matter what. Do they always agree with me? No. Are they loving, loyal, faithful, and true to me at all times? Yes. Do they help me through rough times? Absolutely. They are like an anchor in life's storms.

THE WAY TO BUILD A WISE, GODLY FRIENDSHIP

How can you build a wise friendship that is grounded on godly principles? There are many ways—let me give you ten of them. None of these ways should be isolated from the others. A friendship is built upon a composite of factors.

1. A Shared Faith in Christ Jesus

Deep friendships develop best when two people share faith in Christ Jesus. It is very difficult for two people to become deep, intimate friends if one person is a believer and the other is not. Faith in Christ Jesus is the strongest bond two people can share.

Two people are likely to become better friends if they not only have a shared belief in Jesus as Savior, but if they also have the same level of commitment to following Christ, hold to the same general doctrinal beliefs, share similar spiritual experiences, and desire to learn from and to apply God's Word.

Some of the closest friendships I have observed are among people who have attended the same Sunday school class or Bible study group for years, even decades. These friends tend to be active in other outreaches and opportunities for fellowship in the church—they not only share a mutual faith in Jesus Christ, but they enjoy serving the Lord together.

2. Mutual Interests

Deep friendships develop when two people share mutual interests. A mutual interest may be golf, fishing, hunting, financial investments, family life, a particular type of music, or another sport, hobby, interest, or aspect of one's career. Some of my closest personal friends are fellow photographers. We have a mutual interest that has many facets to it, including the travel involved in photographic excursions, the technology of the equipment, conferences or seminars on photographic techniques, the subject matter we enjoy photographing, and experiences we have had while taking photographs.

If two people have more than one area of common interest, their friendship likely will be even stronger.

3. A Willingness to Give More Than Receive

Deep friendships develop when each person in the relationship seeks to meet the other person's needs more than to have his needs met. If you enter into a friendship with a perspective, "Let me see what this person can do for me," you are going to find yourself disappointed and frustrated. On the other hand, if you enter into a friendship with the attitude, "Let me see what I can give to this person," you likely are going to experience satisfaction and a high degree of personal fulfillment in the relationship.

Those who are takers more than givers tend to be self-centered, selfish people. They also tend to be the quickest to bail out of the relationship if times get tough or the relationship develops conflict.

At times, people enter into friendships because they are personally ambitious. They want what they believe the other person can do for them to promote their status, fame, or power. If you are seeking to develop a friendship with a person because you believe that person will help you accomplish a specific personal goal . . . beware. You are setting yourself up for discouragement, disappointment, and disillusionment.

A true friend is one who loves sacrificially—who gives and expects nothing in return. A true friend is one who may have personal needs, but doesn't mention them continually. A true friend is one who does not need to have his way all the time, but rather, is willing to yield his preferences to the preferences of another person. Read what the apostle Paul wrote:

> Be filled with the Spirit, speaking to one another in psalms and hymns and spiritual songs . . . giving thanks always for all things to God the Father in the name of our Lord Jesus Christ, *submitting to one another in the fear of God*. (Eph. 5:18–21, emphasis added)

> Be kindly affectionate to one another with brotherly love, *in honor giving preference to one another*. (Rom. 12:10, emphasis added)

Godly relationships are those in which there is a willingness to say, "I don't have to have things my way all the time. I'm willing to submit my desires to your desires, my preferences to your preferences." Certainly we are never called to compromise our values, our faith in Christ Jesus, or with evil. We also are never to give up our entire identity just to please another person or to become a doormat on which he walks. We are, however, to mature to the point that we are more concerned about what happens to another person than we are concerned about what happens to us. We are willing to allow our friends the freedom of expression, and we are willing to value their choices, their ideas, and their desires.

That means, in a practical way, that we spend an evening together doing what the other person wants to do. We go out to eat at the restaurant of their choice. We choose to vacation at the destination they desire. We purchase the item in the color they like. And so forth. And all along the way, we do not feel any less a person in yielding our preferences.

I have lived alone now for a number of years, and I know from firsthand experience that God can bring a person to the place where he or she does not feel personally needy for another person's approval or love in order to feel valuable or worthy. Hear me closely on this. I am not saying that the Lord brings us to a place where we no longer need, desire, or bene-fit from other people. No! God desires for us to be in mutually beneficial giving-and-taking relationships. What I have learned is that the Lord can heal our emotions from the inside out so that we no longer feel driven by our own neediness. Those who have low self-worth very often seek out friends or seek to marry because they need someone by their side or on their arm to give them self-confidence, self-value, self-worth, or self-esteem. The Lord desires that we look to Him—not to another person—for our feelings of adequacy, sufficiency, content-ment, worthiness, and value.

If you enter any relationship with the feeling "I must have this person" or "I must be in relationship with this person" . . . you are entering the relationship with a focus on yourself, not the other person. Look at what you would like to be able to give to the other person—what would you like to be able to do for him or her, how would you like to bless his or her life? Deep friendships are formed when both friends are givers more than takers.

Let me assure you . . .

No man can ever meet all the needs in any woman's life.

No woman can ever meet all the needs in any man's life.

No friend can ever meet all the needs in any friend's life.

But the good news is this: The Lord Jesus Christ can meet all the needs in your life so that you are better able to minister to and befriend another person.

4. A WILLINGNESS TO RISK PAIN OR REJECTION

Deep friendships develop when both people in the relationship are willing to risk rejection and pain. Every relationship has the potential for hurt feelings, rejection, and sorrow. If you are waiting to form a close friendship with someone you believe will never hurt you or cause you pain . . . you will never form a deep, intimate friendship. Every person alive has failures, flaws, and weaknesses, and each of us brings our own into our relationships. There is no perfect relationship because a perfect relationship would involve two perfect people, and no such people exist.

Every friendship hits times when communication is not the best, the amount of time spent together is not the most, or shared experiences are not the richest. That's life. It may not be the intent of either person—but it happens nonetheless.

Jesus and Peter were close friends, but that does not mean they didn't hurt each other. Peter no doubt felt hurt when Jesus told him that he was acting like the devil; Jesus no doubt felt hurt when Peter denied knowing Him three times. Did

Peter and Jesus remain friends, however, all the way through the Cross, Resurrection, and Ascension? Yes!

5. Vulnerability to Each Other

Deep friendships develop when both people in the relationship are willing to be vulnerable to each other and share their hearts with transparency. They must be willing to share fully how they are feeling or what they are thinking, without fear of criticism or rejection.

Intimate friendship requires a large amount of trust. Perhaps the most vital building block in any godly relationship is trust. You should be able to trust a friend to keep your confidences, hold your secrets, be loyal to you in a difficult situation, and refuse to turn away from you even if you are persecuted. In turn, you must be a trustworthy friend. Mutual trust is the glue that holds relationships together.

The cornerstone of trust is truthfulness. Absolute honesty is required between friends. If you discover that you have not told the truth to a friend, be quick to apologize and set the matter straight. Above all, you need to tell the truth about yourself. Don't make up a tale about your own background or experience to try to impress a friend. Don't lie about other relationships in your life. Don't whitewash your mistakes or exaggerate your successes. Be truthful. Your telling the truth to a friend gives your friend permission to tell you the truth about himself or herself—and that's the only way you are ever going to get to know each other at a deeper level.

There have been times in my life in which I shared my heart

fully with someone I considered to be a friend, holding nothing back, only to have that person clam up and share nothing of his life in return. When that happens, feelings of fear, self-doubt, and suspicion can develop very quickly, and a friendship can begin to disintegrate rapidly. Deep friendship requires a mutuality of vulnerability.

In my opinion, the two main reasons that so many friendships are shallow are because people are reluctant to be transparent, and because they cannot handle the honest sharing of others. The walls go up almost immediately. The person says, usually by expressions and body language more than words, "I don't trust you enough to be totally honest with you. I'm afraid you will trample on my feelings." Or the person conveys, "Don't tell me too much. I can't handle it. I don't want to know about your pain or disappointment—I'm afraid of feeling partially responsible for your life."

Keep in mind that when you shut others out, you shut yourself in. In close friendship, a person needs to feel that he can say anything without the other person walking away in disgust or disillusionment. No two people are ever going to agree fully on everything. There must be room in a friendship for discussion and debate. There must be a feeling that the friendship is stronger than any disagreement that may arise. Genuine friends confront each other, however, in an attitude of love, helping each other to grow in Christ Jesus and to reach their maximum potential.

No person is strong all the time.

No person is correct all the time.

No person is perfect all the time.

And no person says just the right things all the time.

6. An Attitude of Service

Deep friendships develop when each person in the relationship is willing to serve the other person gladly. We are very reluctant to use the word *serving* in our society. We have associated it with weakness or a lack of status. In a genuine, intimate friendship, however, there is a spontaneous willingness to serve. A true friend looks for ways to serve, to help, to give.

Never lose sight of the fact that Jesus served His disciples. He said,

> He who is greatest among you shall be your servant.
> (Matt. 23:11)

> He who is greatest among you, let him be as the younger,
> and he who governs as he who serves. (Luke 22:26)

Many years ago, there was a man who wanted to be my friend and I wanted to be his friend. But the truth is, I didn't know how to be a friend to this man. He tried his best to be my friend, but I couldn't accept the things he did to serve me and give to me. I had built a wall of self-sufficiency to hide my feelings of inadequacy and my personal pain, and I couldn't handle his overtures of help. The friendship that might have developed never developed . . . and it was my fault.

To be a friend, you must be willing to receive the service

another person renders to you. When two people love to serve each other, they find it easy to respect each other, open up their hearts to each other, and live in harmony with each other.

7. A WILLINGNESS TO FORGIVE FREELY AND QUICKLY

Deep friendships develop when both people in the relationship freely forgive and are quick to ask for forgiveness. If you cannot readily say to another person, "I was only looking out for myself, I wasn't sensitive to you, I'm ashamed of my behavior, and I'm asking you to forgive me," . . . you cannot build a deep and godly friendship with that person.

We all are going to make mistakes from time to time and hurt others inadvertently in the process. Forgiveness is the only way to bring genuine healing to a harmed relationship so that both people can move forward in the relationship with freedom and strength.

"But," you may say, "I'm not the one at fault. Are you telling me I should still ask for forgiveness?"

Yes.

When it comes to restoration and reconciliation of a relationship, it's not a matter of who asks for forgiveness first, but rather, that forgiveness is given and received. There's no standing on pride and saying, "I'm waiting for the other person to apologize." The fact is, you likely are very sorry that there has been a breach in your relationship, no matter who initiated it, and it is wise to say, "I'm sorry that our relationship has been damaged. Please forgive me for what I have done to hurt our friendship. My relationship with you is very valuable to me, and I don't want to be estranged from you." It is better to ask for forgiveness than to stand on a principle of being right and allow a friendship to be damaged.

If a person says, "I forgive you, but . . . " or "I can forgive you for everything, but . . . ," that "but" cancels out the forgiveness. Genuine forgiveness prohibits any harboring of bitterness or resentment. If you continue to allow a situation to fester in your mind . . . if you continue to bring up old wounds and hurts . . . if you continue to feel rejected and isolated . . . then you haven't genuinely forgiven the other person.

No Christian has justification for refusing forgiveness to another person. Remember all that the Lord has forgiven in your life! How many sinful attitudes and actions has He forgiven you? How many times has He forgiven you for repeated offenses against His commandments? How many times has He forgiven you a lack of spiritual sensitivity, an error in judgment, a wasted opportunity, a damaging remark, or a careless comment? How many times has He forgiven you your failure to appreciate Him fully, acknowledge Him frequently, or praise Him fervently?

Jesus taught, "Freely you have received, freely give" (Matt. 10:8). Forgiveness surely has been received freely on our part—we must be quick to offer it freely to others.

8. ACCEPTANCE OF BOTH CRITICISM AND PRAISE

Deep friendships develop when both people in the relationship can accept criticism and offer praise gladly. True friends give each other constructive, helpful, loving criticism, and they also rejoice in each other's successes and accomplishments. The challenge is usually twofold—we must be willing to receive criticism that is offered in a helpful, loving manner, and we must be able to applaud the efforts of our friends. Most of us are far quicker to make critical comments than we are to receive or give constructive criticism. Many of us find it easier to receive compliments than to feel sincere appreciation for the successes of our friends.

If you are willing to accept the praise of your friend, you must be equally willing to accept his criticism. You must be as willing to hear "You are right" as you are to hear "You are wrong."

Constructive criticism is not criticism with the intent of tearing down another person, but rather, it is offered as a way of helping and loving another person. Constructive criticism should always be offered after prayerful consideration—far too often, quick criticism is damaging, hurtful criticism. Constructive criticism should always be offered at a time when the other person can best receive it. Wait a while after the game, after the performance, after the service, after the conversation—wait until the emotional heat has cooled off.

When it comes to criticism, you as the giver of criticism should feel more pain than what you think the receiver of the criticism should feel. It should be just as difficult—or more so—for you to offer criticism than for another person to hear it.

If a genuine friend begins to criticize you, the wise response is to keep your mouth shut, listen intently, and then offer your thanks for their help. Avoid overreacting or justifying your behavior. At times, an explanation about your motives or feelings may be helpful, but avoid being defensive. By all means, avoid raising your voice. Reflect upon what your friend has said to you—you are likely to find a real kernel of truth in what they have shared, and you will benefit as you take their criticism to heart and make some changes in your behavior or attitude.

9. An Adherence to Biblical Principles

Deep and lasting friendships are developed when the friendship is based upon scriptural principles. Can you say to your friend, "Let's allow the principles of God's Word to govern our relationship—the way we speak to each other, the way we treat each other, and what we expect from each other, both in public and in private"? If so, you are on the right footing in your friendship.

10. Proven over Time

Deep and lasting friendships are developed over time. No genuine friendship is built in a day . . . or a week . . . or a month . . . or even a year. Deep and lasting friendships require an expenditure of time—friends must spend both quality of time and quantity of time together conversing and sharing experiences. It is only over time that the other aspects of friendship are established, tested, and refined.

It takes time for trust to build so that each of you can feel transparent and risk vulnerability in your communication. It takes time for each of you to see that the other person's faith and commitment to God's principles are firm. It takes time for each of you to see that the other person's giving is without manipulation and your receiving is without self-centered pride. It takes time to learn another person's interests, wishes, and needs . . . so that you might better help or serve that person.

It takes time to know that a friend is going to be there for you in good times and bad. It takes time to test your mutual ability to forgive and be forgiven, and to weather times of unintentional pain and sorrow.

Don't expect a friendship to be instantaneous.

Don't expect a friendship to last forever with no effort on your part.

Don't expect a friendship to be so resilient that you can ignore it, abuse it, or devalue it without causing damage to the friendship.

For every one of the other facets of deep friendship discussed in this chapter, consistency and constancy over time must be hallmarks of the relationship.

The deep and godly friendships you establish in God's wisdom have a glorious reward: They are going to be eternal friendships. The friendships you establish and build in Christ Jesus are truly the friendships that last forever and produce lasting joy.

EIGHT BASIC BUILDING BLOCKS FOR DEEP FRIENDSHIP

Deep, constant, godly friendships don't just "happen." They are built. There are eight essential building blocks required.

BUILDING BLOCK #1: TIME

You must be willing to spend time with your friends. I must admit, I probably have lost some friends through the years because I have said, "I don't have time," when they invited me to go places or share experiences with them. The more honest truth is—I didn't choose to make the time. We all tend to make time for the things we want to do. We must also make time for the relationships we desire to have.

When we don't have time for our friends, we likely aren't valuing our friends as we should. We also must be aware that we have only so much time in life, and we likely have only the necessary time for a handful of genuine deep friendships. That does not mean we can't have more casual friendships—but for a truly deep friendship to develop, time together is a vital ingredient.

BUILDING BLOCK #2: TALK

A second building block to a good relationship is talk. Conversation is the way you discover more about a person—it is a window through which to peer into another person's heart, mind, soul, and spirit. The more you converse with a person and see inside that person, the more you know about the person. And the more you know about a person, the more you love him or her—or perhaps, the more you realize that your friendship is likely to be short-lived.

Through the years I've heard countless wives say about their husbands, "I just wish he'd talk to me." The fact is—these wives wanted to know their husbands better. They wanted to know what their husbands were thinking and feeling. When a man doesn't talk to his wife, he puts up a barrier to her understanding him. Husband . . . take time to talk to your wife. You may not feel a need to talk, but she needs to hear you talk!

When you are with a friend, the topic of your conversation doesn't really matter. I meet regularly on Saturday mornings to have breakfast with three of my buddies. We go to the same restaurant every Saturday—in fact, the restaurant personnel are so accustomed to our coming that they set aside a certain table just for us.

These three men are in professions different from mine, but we have many common interests. What do we discuss? Anything and everything. We talk about whatever pops into our minds. Our conversation is free-flowing, easy, and natural—no subject is off-limits, no topic is too trivial or too big. We are open with one another. We are friends.

BUILDING BLOCK #3: SHARED TEARS AND LAUGHTER

Genuine friends cry together and laugh together. If a person is a genuine friend, you should have no hesitation whatsoever in going to that person when you are hurt, rejected, or disappointed . . . or when you have a triumphant moment!

Those who stuff all of their emotions—both sorrow and joy—do damage to their own physical health. We all need the "release" of tears and laughter in order to vent our emotions.

BUILDING BLOCK #4: EXPRESSED THANKFULNESS

A friend voices thanksgiving for his or her friends. Not too long ago, one of my friends showed up just when I needed someone to talk to about a situation I was facing. I said to him, "You have an uncanny way of showing up just when I need a listening ear and feel the need to pour out my heart. I'm thankful for you in my life. I'm thankful for the direction and wise counsel you give me!" And I am.

I have a photographer friend who calls me about once a week. I'm never quite sure where he'll be when he calls—one of his recent calls was from Paris. I can always count on his saying two things to me at some point in the call: "I'm grateful to God for our friendship" and "I love you, brother." To have a friend who will openly and frequently make those two statements is a wonderful thing! If you haven't told a friend lately that you are grateful to God for his presence in your life . . . or if you haven't said, "I love you," to a friend . . . I encourage you to do so.

BUILDING BLOCK #5: THOUGHTFUL GESTURES

Sometimes the best way to show your appreciation for a friend is to do something for your friend or give something to your friend. The deed or item need not be grandiose or extravagant—rather, something that conveys the message, "I'm thinking of you. I listen to you. I know what you like—yes, even what you need." A friend takes joy in giving something that he knows his friend desires.

One of my friends is a tremendous giver. He is always sending me something that he thinks I'll enjoy—since he travels a lot and we have a number of common interests, his gifts are always meaningful to me and sometimes rather unusual. As much as I have protested about his gifts to me, he continues to send them. One day he said to me, "I'm just a giver. It's what I do. You can't ever outgive me, so don't even try. I get a lot of joy out of giving. Don't rob me of that joy by telling me not to give."

Husband, does your wife like flowers? Surprise her with a bundle of flowers now and then. Giving her something that you know she likes is a way of saying, "I'm glad you're in my life." Similarly, wife, give your husband something every now and then that is a special surprise, which says, "I am glad you're with me."

A woman told me recently what a friend had done for her. This woman had received word that a family of five was on its way to spend a week at her home while they enrolled their daughter in a nearby college. She had shared news of their impending visit with her friend. The next day, that friend showed up with a large casserole and the comment, "I made extra. I thought you might be able to use this." This woman said, "Now that's a friend! She knew exactly what would bless me most on that particular day."

BUILDING BLOCK #6: TOLERANCE

Friends tolerate the occasional bad mood, the hurtful comment said in haste, or the bad attitude that's the result of being too tired or too stressed out.

Sometimes tolerance means putting up with an annoying habit. Sometimes it means cutting that person some slack when he's fifteen minutes late . . . again. Not long ago, I sat and listened to a friend of mine tell a story I've heard so many times I could tell it in detail myself. This man knew I'd heard the story. Everybody else at the table had heard it. But we all listened as if we were listening for the first time. He's our friend.

BUILDING BLOCK #7: TOUCHING

There's power in appropriate touching between friends. A genuine friend should be someone you feel you can hug, someone you can pat on the back.

A while back, I was eating alone in a restaurant, and I noticed that a certain man in the restaurant was giving his waitress a very hard time about something. Rather than respond in a negative manner, she reached out and touched him lightly on the shoulder and said, "I'm sorry . . ." She didn't have to say anything more. The instant she touched him, he melted—his countenance changed and so did the tone of his voice.

Most people are hungry to be touched—it's a sign to them of care, empathy, concern, appreciation, and value. If a person comes to me after a church service and tells me that he's heartbroken—perhaps his wife has abandoned their family, he has been left alone with their children, and he doesn't know where to turn or what to do—this man doesn't want me to keep my distance and say coldly, "Well, I know God will help you." No. He wants a pastor who will reach out and hug him or put his arm around him and look him in the eye and say, "I hurt for you. I'm going to pray for you and believe for God's best in your life. Let me know if there's anything I can do to help you."

I am certainly not advocating that you hug every person in sight, or that you be overly affectionate with casual acquaintances. You must be sensitive to what another person needs and desires—you should touch another person only in a way you know is comfortable for that person. A friend, however, should be someone that you don't think twice about touching when you desire to express pure, nonsexual affection, comfort, or appreciation.

BUILDING BLOCK #8: TRANSPARENCY

Transparency means not holding deceitful motives, hiding your feelings, or harboring a secret agenda in your dealings with another person. If you are going to develop a genuine friendship with another person, you are going to have to let that person see the real you.

THE SUM IS *LOVE*

All of these building blocks add up to one simple four-letter word: *love*. A person you love is a person you spend time with, talk to, cry with and laugh with, are thankful for, do thoughtful things for, tolerate without complaining, touch with affection, are transparent with, speak the truth to, and trust.

The cardinal principle for having a deep, close, godly friend is to be such a friend.

EIGHT

WISDOM FOR HEALING A DAMAGED RELATIONSHIP

One of the most famous quotes about friendship surely must be this:

> Make new friends but keep the old—
> One is silver and the other gold.

How do we actually do this, however? Every relationship hits snags from time to time. Sometimes relationships are hit with such tremendous pressure that they begin to crumble in seeming irreparable ways. How are we to respond wisely?

There are three major questions that a person must ask when a relationship hits a troubled time:

1. Is this relationship one I want to restore?
2. What caused damage to the relationship?
3. What should we do now?

Your answers to these questions will determine the actions you should take.

A Decision Regarding Restoration and Reconciliation

The first questions you need to ask when a relationship becomes troubled are these: Do I truly want to do whatever is necessary to restore this relationship? Do I value the relationship enough to swallow my pride, to admit my faults, and to make changes? Do I believe the relationship should continue—that it is the right thing before God that I remain in this relationship?

The plain and simple truth is this: Not all friendships are intended to last forever. Some are . . . and some aren't.

People tend to come into your life for a reason, a season, or a lifetime. When you figure out why a person is in your life, you likely will know with more clarity what you might do for that person and how to relate to him.

For-a-Reason Relationships

When someone is in your life for a *reason*, it is usually so that person might meet a need you have expressed, or that you might meet a specific need he has expressed.

God may have sent that person to walk alongside you to assist you through a difficulty, to provide guidance and support to you, or to aid you physically, emotionally, or spiritually. Generally speaking, a person who comes into your life for times such as these appears to be a godsend—and he is! God has sent him just when you need him, for just the length of time you need him.

God may also ask you to be in a person's life for a reason. You may be the one God has chosen to help that person through a difficulty, to provide guidance or support, or to aid the person in a physical, material, emotional, or spiritual way.

Then, without any wrongdoing on your part or the other's part, and likely at a time you can't anticipate in advance, either you or the other person will say or do something to bring the relationship to an end.

Sometimes the other person dies. Sometimes he walks away. Sometimes she acts in a way that forces you to take a stand that she finds unacceptable.

What you must realize is that the reason for that person in your life has been met. The work is done. The prayer—either yours or the other person's—has been answered. And now the time has come to move on.

SEASONAL RELATIONSHIPS

Some people come into your life for a *season*. Generally speaking, this is a season for mutual sharing, growth, or learning from each other. The season may be one that is defined by external circumstances—perhaps the two of you have been assigned to be roommates in a college dorm, or perhaps you are living next door, are working together in the same company, or are part of a parents' group while your children are attending the same school.

Seasonal relationships are likely to be ones that bring you peace, comfort, and camaraderie. Often a person with whom you are in a season of relationship makes you laugh, teaches you something, or gives you valuable insight into life. The person may provide valuable ongoing help to you for a major project, or you may be helpful to the other person during the accomplishment of a mutual goal.

Eventually, in seasonal relationships, one or both parties move on. The person may move from the neighborhood, move from the city, or change jobs, or circumstances in your life may change. Children graduate, interests change, and projects are accomplished.

Enjoy the seasonal relationship! It's real and it's valuable . . . but only for a season.

There is usually sadness associated with the end of a seasonal relationship because the ties are deeper and stronger. Still, we must recognize that God put the person in our lives for a season, and seasons change.

LIFETIME RELATIONSHIPS

Other relationships are intended to be for a lifetime. These relationships are ones in which a person helps teach you lifetime lessons about commitment, friendship, loyalty, and love. The things you discuss and the tasks you undertake together have a solid emotional foundation of caring and mutual give-and-take.

Your role in a lifetime relationship is to accept the lessons, love the person, and put what you learn from this person to use in all other relationships and areas of your life.

Someone once said, "Love is blind, but friendship is clair-voyant." A lifetime friend can see who you are, often more clearly than you can see the reality of your deepest feelings and the underlying reasons for your behaviors. A lifetime friend has the historical context of your friendship against which to weigh your behavior and project consequences from your actions.

CHERISH AND VALUE EACH TYPE OF RELATIONSHIP

Each of these types of friendships is to be cherished and val-ued. We are not to think less, or to love less, the friend who is in our lives for only a reason or a season. Every friend deserves our best effort at friendship and our best efforts at caring, kindness, and courtesy.

There are two times when it is most helpful to recognize whether a relationship is for a reason, a season, or a lifetime—these times are when a relationship reaches a point where a com-mitment is expected or required, and when a relationship ends.

If you are planning to make a vow to someone, make certain you understand the longevity factor associated with the com-mitment you are making. I'm not referring only to marriage, although marriage is certainly a relationship that calls for a commitment in vows. Don't vow to be another person's friend for a lifetime if you can see that the friendship is likely only to be for a reason or a season in your life. Don't commit to a long-term relationship in business, counseling, or caretaking if you suspect your relationship with that person may be only for a season or a specific reason.

Knowing that a relationship is only for a reason, or for a season, also can help us from feeling deeply rejected or wounded when a relationship ends.

WALK AWAY OR STAY?

There are times when we must walk away from a relationship because the person with whom we are in relationship has embarked on a path of rebellion against God, or because that person has threatened our lives, become abusive to us, or in some other way has put the relationship into an unhealthy or sinful state. There are times when God steps in and says about a relationship, "No more."

At other times, we should do our utmost to restore or reestablish a broken relationship. We should do everything we know to do to rebuild the relationship to a point of strength, vibrancy, and health.

If you do not want to restore your damaged relationship, do your best to end the relationship in peace. If both of you are withdrawing from each other, it may be that you can simply let the matter lie. If one person wants to sustain and repair the relationship, however, and the other person does not, you are going to find yourself in conflict. You will be uncomfortable or in emotional turmoil in the other person's presence unless you find a way of resolving the situation and inviting the Lord to bring you both to a place of forgiveness and peace. Don't delay in this. The longer you wait to bring resolution to your relationship, the stronger the pain one or both of you are likely to experience.

If you both truly want to heal your broken relationship, take heart. Virtually any damaged relationship can be healed if both people involved are committed to healing the relationship. It will take intentional effort on the part of both persons. It will take persistence and prayer. It will take patience and extra time and talk. But it is possible.

Ask God to show you how to help your friend to grow in Christ Jesus. Ask God to show you how you should change and grow to become more like Christ Jesus in your character, attitudes, and behavior. Ask God to heal the emotional wounds in each of you. Ask God to show each of you how to be a better friend to the other.

A DISCERNMENT OF WHAT DAMAGED THE RELATIONSHIP

The first step toward restoration and reconciliation is going to be an admission of the breakdown. You both must come to the point where you admit there's a problem in your relationship and you need to make some changes to restore the friendship you once enjoyed.

Then, ask yourselves, "Where did the relationship get off track?"

This is not a time for accusations or self-justification, but rather, a time for objective evaluation of things that need to be changed, clarified, or set right. Avoid thinking or speaking in terms of "you always" or "you never." Focus instead on what specifically was understood or misunderstood . . . what specifically was said or not said . . . what specifically was done or not done that brought injury to the relationship.

We are wise to recognize that some friendships or relationships have never been fully built in the first place. One or more of the building blocks identified in the previous chapter are missing or underdeveloped. If there's a flaw in your relationship, focus on the area.

Recognize, too, that it takes ongoing effort to keep a friendship strong. You can't spend one week with a person and then not see or talk to that person for five years and expect your friendship to be intact. You can't be transparent to a friend in one conversation and then stonewall that friend in your next five conversations and build a strong friendship. Take a look at your own consistency in communicating, giving, sharing, spending time, and expressing thankfulness.

Even a fully built, consistently nurtured friendship, however, can be damaged. No marriage is ever totally beyond the possibility of breakdown . . . no friendship is beyond the possibility of damage.

The foremost way to damage any relationship is simply to undo or tear down one or more of the building blocks identified in Chapter 7. Relationships are impaired or harmed when . . .

- You stop spending time together.

- You stop talking to each other.

- You become reluctant to share your sorrows and your joys—you stop crying together and laughing together.

- You no longer express your thanks or do thoughtful things for each other.

- You become increasingly critical of each other—less and less tolerant of each other's errors, less appreciative of each other's efforts, less accepting of each other's weaknesses.

- You stop touching each other with warmth and tender affection.

- You build a wall and no longer share your life freely with each other—one or both of you hold things back and conceal your motives, feelings, and thoughts.

- One or both of you lie to each other—not only about what you are doing, but what you are thinking and feeling with regard to your relationship.

- You stop trusting each other.

ATTITUDES AND BEHAVIORS THAT STOP THE FLOW OF LOVE

When love stops flowing between friends or spouses, you nearly always are going to find one or more of the following at work:

1. Selfishness. When a person begins to focus on self rather than taking into consideration the other person, the relationship begins to falter. Selfishness very often manifests itself as busyness. When a person becomes extremely preoccupied with what he is doing . . . becomes singularly intent on reaching his personal goals . . . becomes tightly focused only what he wants to do and where he wants to go . . . he shuts out his friends. He occupies himself with things that are more important than his friends, and he sends the signal, "I want to do this more than I want to be with you. I want to achieve this by myself to the exclusion of you in the process." If a friend or spouse feels completely shut out, he or she is likely to walk away.

2. Manipulation. When one person begins to control the other person in a relationship, the relationship begins to crumble. Manipulation takes many forms—for example, playing mind games with a person, verbal belittling or verbal abuse, withholding finances or rewards that are due to a person, withholding sex in a marriage. The goal of manipulation is that one person becomes "master" and the other becomes "slave." The relationship is no longer a mutual friendship among equals, but a hierarchy.

3. Jealousy. When one person becomes so jealous that he refuses to allow the other person to have any other friends or relationships, the relationship begins to disintegrate. I'm not talking about marriage here; there is a godly jealousy that a husband should have for a wife and a wife for a husband so that no other person is allowed into the intimacy of their marriage relationship. Even in marriage, however, each spouse needs to allow the other to have friends. Husbands should have godly male friends; wives should have godly female friends.

4. Constant Criticism. When one person constantly voices disapproval of the way the other person looks, talks, or acts . . . continually disagrees with the other person's choices and decisions . . . or continually denigrates the other person's value or worthiness . . . the relationship crumbles. Certainly a constructive, helpful suggestion from time to time is warranted between friends—but a continual harping on what one person perceives to be the other person's faults, failures, or mistakes is deadly to a relationship.

5. *Explosive Emotional Behavior.* The uncontrolled venting of emotions on the part of one or both persons leads to damage in a relationship. Why? Because when anger or bitterness is vented in an explosive way, very often things are said and pain is inflicted that can never be undone regardless of the number of apologies offered.

There is a way to express anger "without sinning" (Eph. 4:26). We can channel our anger into constructive change—putting the focus on what we can and should do rather than on what we want the other person to do. We can address concerns and problems before they fester to the boiling point. We can share our frustrations and feelings before bitterness or hate reaches the explosion level. We can voice that we are upset, concerned, disappointed, or in pain without raising our voice, digging up the past, or ripping apart another person's identity. And we can always choose to give voice to our emotions without striking out at a person's personal characteristics—appearance, desirability, race, age, cultural background, family upbringing, or character faults.

To vent anger or bitterness in an uncontrolled way nearly always causes a deep gash in another person's self-worth. That gash can be so deep that it marks the end of all love in the relationship.

If you are subject to emotional outbursts, get help. Work with a counselor to discover why you are so angry, bitter, or in such pain.

6. *Covetousness.* Jealousy is holding on to something that you believe is rightfully yours—and that, as in the case of marriage, may be rightfully yours. God was "jealous" for the Israelites because they were rightfully His people. Envy or covetousness, in contrast, is desiring something that rightfully belongs to another person. It is wanting what is the other person's—it may be a physical trait such as strength or beauty, a possession, a talent, a spiritual gift, a ministry, an ability or skill, a relationship, a family background. It may be a coveting of reputation, fame, or position of authority. It is impossible to sustain a friendship with someone who wants what you have and desires to be who you are. Friendship requires a mutuality of respect and admiration for what the other person has, does, and is.

7. *The Introduction of Inappropriate Sexual Intimacy.* Friendship and marriage are two different relationships when it comes to sexual intimacy. Sexual intimacy has no place in friendship—it belongs solely in marriage. Certainly a friendship can grow to the point where romance blossoms and marriage results. But even then, sexual intimacy needs to be reserved for marriage. When sexual behavior is introduced into a friendship, the nature of that friendship automatically changes.

This is one of the reasons it is so difficult for men to have women friends and vice versa. It is nearly impossible for a married man to have a female friend or for a married woman to have a male friend—especially if the two people are of the same generation and are healthy physically. The possibility of sexual involvement is always there.

Sexual intimacy does not add to a friendship. Nothing that is contrary to God's commandments can build up a friendship.

8. Expressions of Betrayal or Disloyalty. If one person betrays the other or is overtly disloyal to the other person, the relationship suffers a major blow. This is especially true if a confidence is made public or one person joins forces with others to undermine his friend's efforts. Few things can damage trust as much as an act of betrayal or disloyalty.

There are a number of behaviors that may be classified as a betrayal or as disloyal. Adultery or any act of infidelity can be considered a betrayal. Dishonesty in business dealings can be an act of betrayal. Public accusations and public criticism can be perceived as acts of disloyalty. It doesn't really matter who is right or wrong in such situations—it doesn't really matter if the person who is perpetuating the action claims to have a good motive. What matters is how the person who is injured, exposed, accused, or criticized feels and thinks. Judas no doubt thought he was justified in turning Jesus over to the religious authorities in Jerusalem; he may even have thought that he was helping to further build the case or speed up the timetable for Jesus to be revealed and declared the Messiah. Judas's actions, however, were a betrayal of Jesus—they were acts of disloyalty.

If you have acted without intention, and your friend lets you know he feels betrayed by something you said or did, be quick to apologize. Express your sorrow. Repent of your disloyal behavior. Ask for forgiveness. Don't attempt to justify your behavior because you acted without malice—do what you can to heal the hurt the other person is feeling.

Identifying the Steps That Both Must Take

There are four basic steps that each must take if you choose to heal your damaged relationship.

1. Apologize to Each Other

If the relationship is worth saving, each person should be willing to apologize for his or her part in the misunderstanding, breakdown, or damage. Rarely is a breakdown the result of just one person's actions or words. There is nearly always something that each person said or didn't say, did or didn't do, that contributed to the damage. Even if you think you are totally in the right, apologize. What do you really have to lose if an apology from you can heal a damaged relationship you value?

Genuinely choose to forgive each other for the pain of the broken relationship.

2. Identify Constructive Positive Steps Each Can Take

Deal in specifics. Focus on observable, definitive behaviors that can be readily done in the near future. For example, if you agree that you need to spend more time together, set a time and place or plan an event or vacation that will result in your spending more time together. If you agree that you need to talk more, set aside a time on each of your schedules when you can get together for a relaxed meal and a time of no-agenda, no-time-limit sharing.

3. Make a Mutual Commitment to Rebuild the Relationship

Agree to work on the relationship. If one person says, "I'm finished, I'm gone," recognize that you cannot force another person to stay in relationship with you or to have the kind of relationship you desire. You can't make another person love you or be your friend. Friendship is a choice, an act of the will, as is marriage.

4. Agree to Move Forward and Let the Past Be the Past

Refuse to harbor blame or resentment. Don't bring up past hurts. Don't let your mind dwell on the frustration, sorrow, discouragement, or disappointment you have felt in the past. Face the future with optimism that you are going to be able to restore your relationship and that bright days lie ahead for you both. Think and act positively. Ask God to heal your friendship and make it stronger than ever.

Choose to Grow Personally

A damaged relationship can provide an excellent opportunity for personal introspection, healing, and growth. Choose to focus on what you can learn from your experience in a relationship. Here are five very important questions I encourage you to reflect upon:

1. Am I projecting onto my friend or spouse a hurt or sorrow that happened to me in the past? Were you abused as a child or teenager? Were you once rejected or abandoned by someone you loved? Were you deeply hurt, mistreated, or betrayed by someone years ago?

Very often we carry old hurts into new relationships. We carry old patterns of responding or reacting into new friendships.

2. Am I projecting onto my friend or spouse what is actually true in my own life? It takes a great deal of personal objectivity to answer this question honestly because we usually do not see clearly our own failures or weaknesses. Rather, we have a tendency to project onto another person the thoughts and feelings that we secretly hold ourselves. If we are stingy . . . we tend to criticize another person for a lack of generosity. If we are harboring a lot of inner anger . . . we tend to criticize what we perceive to be anger in the other person.

We also have a tendency to project onto another person the thoughts and feelings that we hold to be true about ourselves. If we see ourselves as having little value, we tend to treat other people as if they have little value. If we feel we are failing, we tend to look for points of failure or error in other people.

Take a long, hard look at the criticisms you are leveling at another person. Are these actually areas in which you fear that you are personally failing? Are you pointing out the sins in another person's eyes without recognizing that you are guilty of the same sin?

3. Am I afraid of intimacy with another person? Are you afraid of having a close relationship? Do you feel a need for more personal space? Do you feel violated if a person begins to understand you too well? Do you feel suspicious if a person seems to like you too much?

The old saying is true: It is better to have loved and lost than never to have loved at all. It is better to have a close friend and lose that friend, than never to have had a friend at all. Take the risk of love.

4. Do I have unfounded expectations for this relationship? Are you expecting more than the other person is able to give? There are some people who have a tremendous amount of love to give and who are quick and generous in expressing their feelings . . . and there are some people who have very little to give and are slow and reluctant to express their love. Some people have abundant happiness and peace in their lives, and they are very confident in building relationships. Others are not. In fact, there are some people who simply don't know how to love. They don't have the capacity to be readily warm, generous, available, or transparent. Be realistic in your expectations. It will be far easier for you to adjust your expectations than to change the other person! You likely will have to love more, forgive more, and communicate more—with few returns at the outset.

5. Are the feelings of rejection you are experiencing actual rejection, or are they feelings of low self-worth that you don't deserve to be accepted and loved? There are some people who have such low self-esteem that they don't believe anybody is capable of loving them. They therefore build a wall of unworthiness. Rather than see the wall they have built, however, they view the other person's failure to break through the wall as rejection. Be honest with yourself. Are you capable of receiving the love someone else desires to express to you?

HEALING CAN BE STRENGTHENING

God never simply restores a broken person or relationship to what was. He continually calls us to move from strength to strength. As you follow God's wisdom for healing your damaged relationship, look for the changes you build into your relationship to strengthen your relationship. Work at reconciliation with the hope and the intent that your relationship will be more vibrant, more resilient, more mutually beneficial, and more purposeful. What God heals, God uses to bring glory to His name.

NINE

WISDOM IN TIMES OF CONFLICT AND CRITICISM

A couple of years ago, I was harshly criticized by a nationally recognized Christian leader for something that had happened in my personal life. His comments, which were printed nationally, were very hurtful to me personally. I came to know in a very real way what Jesus meant when He used the phrase, "If ye have ought against any" (Mark 11:25 KJV).

Although this isn't the exact definition of that term in King James English, my definition is true to the meaning: When we have ought against a brother, we find ourselves saying such things as . . .

- "He ought to have behaved differently toward me."

- "He ought not to have said that about me."

- "He ought to have drawn different conclusions about my situation."

- "He ought to have kept his opinions about me and my future to himself."

What did I do with these feelings of "ought"—these feelings against my brother in Christ?

First, I called this man. I felt strongly that I needed to let him know that he had hurt me by his comments. He did not receive my first two calls but finally, I got him on the phone. I quickly realized that he had spoken without knowing any of the real facts of the situation. He had made a judgment without due process. He had self-appointed himself to be my prosecutor, judge, and jury.

I asked him why he hadn't let me know that he had felt offended by what had happened in my life. I asked him why he hadn't called me prior to making such hurtful comments about me in the public media. He had no answer.

Furthermore, he expressed no regret whatsoever for the pain he had caused me personally or professionally. I hung up the phone disappointed and, frankly, a little stunned. But I also hung up the phone knowing that I had done what was biblically correct. I had gone to this man with my personal grievance.

The next step I took was to forgive this man and let the matter drop. I didn't speak out against him or seek to retaliate, justify myself, or point out his errors. I refuse even now to tell who he was or what he said, or to discuss the situation that prompted his criticism. I let go of the anger, frustration, and hurt that I felt, and I said to the Lord, "He is

Your concern. I trust You to deal with him in whatever way You choose."

How do you feel when you are criticized? Do you feel sad, angry, hurt, insecure, exposed, betrayed? How do you respond? Do you blame, accuse, stuff your emotions, or apologize?

Conflict is part of every person's life. It is found at home, work, school, in the neighborhood, between friends, at sports arenas, and yes, even in the church. We can't escape conflict. Rather, we need to learn how to deal with it and respond to it. In nearly all cases, conflict, misunderstanding, and criticism go together, at least to a degree.

THREE BASIC TRUTHS ABOUT CONFLICT

Many people would like to live in a totally conflict-free world. Their idea of paradise is a world without any criticism, any difference of opinion, any argument or debate. I assure you, such a world is not going to be established this side of heaven.

Let me share with you three basic truths about conflict:

1. CONFLICT CANNOT BE AVOIDED

Conflict can never be avoided completely. If conflict could have been avoided, Jesus certainly would have chosen a different route. So would Paul and all of the first apostles of Jesus. God never promises any person a life free of conflict. He never commands us to avoid conflict. Rather, God admonishes us to learn how to respond to conflict in a godly manner.

2. CONFLICT AMONG EQUALS
IS NOT INEVITABLE

Even though conflict can never be fully avoided, it is not inevitable among rivals or equals. Some people assume that just because two people are equal in their talents or achievements, they must be rivals or be in open conflict with each other. That isn't at all the case. In fact, as Christians we are to live in harmony with our fellow believers. We are not to set ourselves up to be in competitive conflict.

In the early days of our nation, two giants of the faith, John Wesley and George Whitefield, led major revival movements that resulted in thousands of people accepting Christ as their Savior. One day a man asked John Wesley if he thought he would see George Whitefield in heaven. Wesley replied, "No, I do not." The man asked again, "Are you telling me that you don't believe George Whitefield is a converted man?"

Wesley replied, "I do not believe that I will see him in heaven, because he will be so close to the throne, and I will be so far away that I will never see him."

Although they disagreed doctrinally, these two men refused to criticize each other or to engage in personal conflict. Neither man gave evidence of being motivated by envy of the other.

3. ALL CONFLICT IS NOT SIN

At times, conflict arises through simple neglect or an innocent mistake. Not all conflict is rooted in willful behavior. Furthermore, conflict can result in something good. As people discuss the reasons for their conflict, more understanding and appreciation for each other can develop. New creative approaches can be identified as people share their differing perspectives and ideas.

The Bible says, "As iron sharpens iron, so a man sharpens the countenance of his friend" (Prov. 27:17).

Iron sharpens iron through conflict—iron pieces grate against each other to produce a sharp edge. It is through lively, honest, friendly debate, discussion, and argument that our opinions are honed, our thinking becomes clear, and we become more aware of our own beliefs. Friends challenge friends to grow in faith, to be bolder in their witness, and to pursue excellence.

OUR RESPONSE TO CONFLICT AND CRITICISM

Although we will never be able to stop or control completely a flow of conflict or criticism, we can determine how we will choose to respond to our critics and those who seek to be our enemies.

MAKE HEALING, GROWTH, AND RESOLUTION THE GOAL

Our goal as Christians should always be to bring healing and peaceful resolution in times of conflict. We are to be peacemakers. This is true not only for conflicts that arise between believers, but also for conflicts that erupt between a believer and a nonbeliever. It is up to the Christian to take the lead in

seeking a peaceful resolution to a disagreement. The nonbeliever has neither an understanding of genuine inner peace nor
motivation to work for peaceful resolution.

If you approach conflict as an opportunity to fight for your
cause, to gain vengeance, or to make a statement of self-justification, you are likely to increase the conflict, not decrease it.

When conflict erupts, ask immediately for the Lord to give
you an attitude of humility and to help you make peace your goal.

BE REALISTIC ABOUT THE EMOTIONAL IMPACT

Be realistic about how conflict affects you. The apostle Paul
no doubt was sorrowful and discouraged when he learned that
people would preach the gospel with a wrong motive (Phil.
1:15–17). Even so, Paul refused to wallow in self-pity or
engage in an argument. He chose instead to see the big picture—the result was that the gospel was being preached. He
rejoiced in that! In fact, he made rejoicing a conscious decision.
Paul wrote, "I rejoice, yes, and will rejoice" (Phil. 1:18).
Regardless of how he may have felt personally, he chose to
maintain an attitude of contentment, gratitude, and joy.

Be realistic about how you habitually tend to respond to
conflict. Some people routinely respond to conflict in very
unhealthy ways:

- They suppress their feelings. They deny the impact the
  conflict is having on them. They stuff all emotions they
  feel—they deny them or dismiss them completely.

- They repress their feelings. They acknowledge the conflict and their feelings, but they refuse to express their feelings or opinion. Rather, they keep quiet in the hope that the conflict will dissipate, and they can avoid an open confrontation or discussion.

- They are quick to blame and accuse in retaliation. They refuse to accept any part in the conflict.

The person who makes these responses is usually very insecure. He does not want a genuine resolution of a conflict, only a quick fix that causes the immediate pain of the moment to cease.

The problem with all of these approaches is that they produce no clear-cut end to the conflict. Those who repress and suppress their emotions only put their feelings on hold. Feelings that are stifled do not dissipate naturally. Rather, they simmer, soak, ferment, and grow inside a person, and one day they will explode or manifest themselves in sickness. Bitterness and resentment are likely. And the end result of bitterness and resentment is anything but positive: the loss of precious relationships, a loss of joy, a stunting of spiritual growth, and a growing ineffectiveness in one's ability to minister to others.

Check your own response to conflict. If you are dealing with conflict and criticism in a negative way, change your approach!

SEEK OUT THE CAUSE OF THE CONFLICT

Seek to identify the cause of the conflict. Ask yourself:

- Was it something I said?

- Was it the tone of voice I used?

- Has there been a breakdown in communication?

- Is the conflict rooted in a deep emotional problem or need in the other person?

- Is the conflict the result of the other person's drive toward perfectionism?

At times the root of the conflict is an honest difference in opinion. Conflict sometimes involves different perspectives on a situation or different ideas about how to proceed in a matter. At times, however, conflict is rooted in jealousy, envy, manipulation, or a power grab. The apostle Paul had no doubt as to the cause of the conflict that arose in the church after his imprisonment in Rome. He identified the two main causes as being envy and strife.

Generally speaking, the four most common causes for conflict are these:

1. A Failure in Communication. Conflict is sometimes rooted in a failure to communicate clearly. When I really want to make sure that I have been heard correctly, I ask a person, "What is it that you heard me say? What is it that you think I meant?" Very often, the person says something back to me that is not precisely what I said or what I meant. It's better to clarify communication immediately rather than let a matter proceed in error. Errors in communication usually do not resolve themselves automatically—over time, they tend to create more problems, not fewer problems.

2. Emotional Baggage and Projection. Yet another cause for conflict can be a person's emotional baggage. If a person grows up in an abusive environment, he is prone to respond to life with a defensive posture aimed at self-protection. Any statement that comes close to sounding like a hurtful message he heard as a child is likely to trigger an angry, self-justifying response . . . or perhaps a wall of stone silence. Opinions and motivations, which may be far from the truth, are projected onto the speaker. The result can be conflict.

3. Perfectionism. Perfectionism can be a root cause of conflict. A genuine perfectionist cannot accept responsibility for anything that is less than perfect. He cannot admit he is wrong or has erred. Therefore, when something goes awry, the perfectionist tends to become defensive, accusatory, or angry. Conflict is the result.

4. Pride. Perhaps the most insidious cause of conflict is pride. There's nothing wrong about being wrong occasionally. But the person who is proud cannot admit he is wrong. The proud person cannot bring himself to say, "I'm sorry" . . . "please forgive me" . . . or "I made a mistake." The proud person limits his potential to grow because a significant amount of growth comes as we learn from our mistakes. The proud person lives in a world in which he feels compelled to defend and maintain his position as "number one." Conflict with others is always a consequence.

YOU CAN'T CHANGE ALL CAUSES OF CONFLICT

Let me quickly point out that you can't help a person who doesn't want to be helped. You can't force a perfectionist to change his ways. You can't force a proud person to lay down his pride. You can't cause a person to seek healing for damaged emotions if that person doesn't want to be healed or sees no need for healing. You can't insist that another person lay down hatred, resentment, and bitterness. You can't require another person to forgive. And therefore, you can't change all causes of conflict or erase all criticism.

Rather than become frustrated at your failure to "fix" the other person in the conflict, focus on what can be done to move forward together in a peaceful way. Don't accuse the other person of being proud, emotionally ill, or a perfectionist—such an accusation will only enlarge the problem. Instead, focus on what you can do solely in yourself.

YOUR PERSONAL INNER RESPONSE

There are at least ten things you can do to create a positive response to a conflict and set the stage for peaceful resolution. These are all things you can do individually and personally, without any participation from the other person in the conflict:

1. Refuse to respond in anger. Choose to adopt and maintain a quiet spirit. No matter what another person says or does, refuse to throw a fit or erupt in frustration. If you have a "short fuse," get a longer one!

2. Make no attempt to defend yourself immediately. Let all the criticism and furor blow over. There may be a time later in which you need to state your case, but until that time comes, keep quiet. When the time for your defense comes, ask the

Holy Spirit to tell you what to say. Jesus promised His disciples, "The Holy Spirit will teach you in that very hour what you ought to say" (Luke 12:12).

3. Ask the Holy Spirit to put a seal on your lips and to put a guard on your mouth. Make your prayer in a time of conflict the prayer that David prayed:

> Set a guard, O LORD, over my mouth;
> Keep watch over the door of my lips. (Ps. 141:3)

4. If after calm reflection you still find yourself totally puzzled as to what created a conflict, ask the Holy Spirit to reveal to you the cause. One of the gifts that the Holy Spirit generously bestows on those who request it is discernment. The Holy Spirit does not want you to wander about in confusion— He wants you to know all you need to know to respond to a situation with love, joy, peace, patience, kindness, mercy, and self-control.

5. Regardless of how a conflict arises, see the conflict as coming from God. I'm not saying that the Lord sent or caused the conflict, but He allowed it. And therefore, it comes from Him for a purpose in your life. That purpose is ultimately for your good—for your refinement, strengthening, preparation, and learning. If you see a conflict as having a godly purpose, you are going to be far less likely to lash out at the other person. Rather, you are going to be more willing to forgive, slower to react, and more willing to make changes in your own attitudes and behavior.

6. Ask the Holy Spirit, "Is this my fault?" Ask the Holy Spirit to reveal very specifically any part that you played in bringing about the conflict. If He shows you something that you did to cause or enlarge the conflict, don't run from your responsibility. Admit your fault; ask for forgiveness; make a commitment to change your conduct. Say to the other person, "Is there something you can suggest to me to help me avoid creating a conflict like this in the future?" Give the person an opportunity to vent fully. And as he does, listen closely. There may be a nugget of valuable help in what he says to help you become a more godly person.

7. Forgive the other person. No matter what has happened or what has been said, forgive. We do not have the right as Christians to harbor unforgiveness.

I have heard people say on occasion, "Well, there are some things that just can't be forgiven." Like what? What is it that Jesus couldn't forgive in your life? What is it that Jesus says is beyond His ability to cleanse, heal, restore, or forgive in a person? Take another look at your own past. If God has forgiven you . . . He expects you to be able to forgive yourself. If God has forgiven you . . . He expects you to extend that forgiveness to others. Jesus said,

> Therefore be merciful, just as your Father also is merciful. Judge not, and you shall not be judged. Condemn not, and you shall not be condemned. Forgive, and you will be forgiven. (Luke 6:36–37)

Forgiveness does not mean denying that you were hurt or that the matter was important. Rather, forgiveness means letting go and letting God. It means turning another person over to God's judgment. It means trusting God to deal with a person as God chooses, without putting yourself in the way.

It doesn't make any difference if the other person asks for forgiveness or not. Forgive. Your forgiveness should not be withheld pending the other's repentance.

Forgive quickly. The sooner you forgive, the sooner you can receive God's healing for any pain or sorrow you have experienced. God's Word tells us,

> Let all bitterness, wrath, anger, clamor, and evil speaking be put away from you, with all malice. And be kind to one another, tenderhearted, forgiving one another, even as God in Christ forgave you. (Eph. 4:31–32)

8. Begin immediately to treat the other person with genuine kindness and tenderness. Look for a way that you can express love to the other person. Speak well of the person. Find a way to help the person. Pray for the person.

9. Choose to learn something from the conflict. Ask the Holy Spirit, "How can I avoid a conflict such as this in the future?" Ask God to reveal to you the lessons He desires for you to learn and the changes He desires for you to make.

10. View the conflict as an opportunity to respond as Christ would respond. Ask the Holy Spirit to minister through you to the other person. Those who respond to a conflict in a godly

manner are strong witnesses for the Lord. You never know who is observing your behavior in a time of criticism or conflict. When you respond without hatred, malice, anger, or bitterness, you send a powerful message about the life-transforming power of God's love and forgiveness.

A POSITIVE RESOLUTION
STARTS WITH A CHOICE

Each of these positive responses to conflict and criticism requires a choice on your part. You must choose to maintain a quiet spirit, keep quiet, avoid self-justification, and forgive. You must choose to ask the Holy Spirit to give you discernment, future direction, and the ability to respond to the other person with Christ's own character traits. You must choose to accept your part in a conflict and then learn and grow and change as a person.

Your choice ultimately must become a commitment to respond to criticism and conflicts wisely, not instinctively. Will you make a commitment today to respond to conflicts and criticism with God's wisdom?

TEN

WISDOM FOR ESTABLISHING THE ULTIMATE RELATIONSHIP

One Sunday when I was twelve years old, I went forward at the close of church service in response to the preacher's invitation to receive Jesus as my Savior. In that hour, I believed in my heart that Jesus had died on the cross for my sins—I believed fully that He had taken my place and had died a sacrificial, atoning, redemptive death on my account so that I would never need to face the consequences for an unredeemed sin nature. I received Jesus into my life.

In that hour, my spiritual past, present, and future were changed forever. My sins were forgiven, all guilt was cleansed completely from my life, my spiritual nature was transformed, and my eternal future in heaven was secured.

In that hour, I established a relationship with God.

THREE PHASES OF OUR RELATIONSHIP WITH GOD

Every relationship with God has the potential for three phases.

THE FIRST PHASE OF OUR RELATIONSHIP WITH GOD: WE RECEIVE JESUS AS SAVIOR

The beginning point of any person's relationship with God is the moment he or she accepts Jesus as Savior.

"But what," you may ask, "about infant baptism, church membership, or the completion of an instructional course on what it means to be a Christian?" Those occasions may mark a person's growing relationship with the church, or with a specific denomination or body of believers, but none of those occasions or ceremonies result in a person having a transformed spirit or receiving the gift of eternal life. The Holy Spirit is sent to dwell within us and to transform our lives at the time we willfully, consciously, intentionally, and actively receive Jesus as our Savior. It is His indwelling presence that secures our new nature . . . secures our eternal life . . . and seals our relationship.

You may be asking, "Do you mean to say I don't have a relationship with God prior to the time I receive Jesus as my Savior?" That's precisely what I mean. Prior to a person's receiving Jesus, he is living in a sinful state. The person may not be a blatant sinner in his actions, but his spirit is unregenerated, unrenewed, "unborn." Every person since the fall of Adam and Eve in the Garden of Eden is born with a sin nature. God will not have a relationship with sin.

What is God's position toward us prior to our acceptance of Jesus as Savior? God is our Creator. He loves us. He extends mercy to us and offers forgiveness to us. He very often protects us and provides for us until we receive Him. He sends His Holy Spirit to convict us of our need for a Savior. But He is not in relationship with us. It is at the foot of the cross that a relationship is established and God becomes our heavenly Father, the merciful Forgiver of our sin and Redeemer of our lives, and we become His full adopted and forgiven children and joint heirs with Christ Jesus of all His blessings.

This is a hard truth for many people to accept, especially those who think that by being good and by amassing a significant number of good deeds they will gain God's favor and enter heaven. Hard or not—this is the truth of God's Word. If you don't believe me, take Jesus at His word: "Most assuredly, I say to you, unless one is born again, he cannot see the kingdom of God" (John 3:3).

I am always amazed at those who reject Jesus. How do they make it through life's difficult times? How do they keep their balance in a world that seems to be in perpetual chaos? How do they sleep at night? How do they face each new day with confidence?

We need Jesus to be our Savior. Every person is born with a sin nature that needs to be transformed and changed—and only God can do that work in us. We cannot forgive ourselves, transform ourselves, or remove our own guilt and shame. John 3:16 declares God's eternal truth: "For God so loved the world that He gave His only begotten Son, that whoever believes in Him should not perish but have everlasting life."

We need the Holy Spirit, whom Jesus sends to live in every

believer. We need the Holy Spirit to guide us into the full truth about Jesus Christ. We need the Holy Spirit to direct our steps daily, and to help us make wise choices and godly decisions. We need the Holy Spirit to remind us of God's commandments and the truth of Jesus Christ so we will know what to do and what to say in any situation in which we find ourselves. We need the Holy Spirit to comfort us when we experience pain and sorrow. We need the Holy Spirit to convict us of our sins and errors so we can repent and make positive changes in our lives. We need the Holy Spirit to defeat evil on our behalf. We need the Holy Spirit to conform us to the image of Christ Jesus. We need the Holy Spirit to make us whole.

Even if you don't think you need God, I tell you today with confidence and boldness: Yes . . . you do need God. Your life will end. You will enter eternity either as a friend of God or as an enemy of God. You will face the consequences for your decision regarding Jesus Christ as God's only begotten Son, sent to this earth to die for our sins so we might be saved.

The first stage of our relationship with God happens in a moment: We believe in and receive Jesus as our Savior. He, in turn, immediately imparts the Holy Spirit to dwell in us.

THE SECOND PHASE OF OUR RELATIONSHIP WITH GOD: WE SERVE JESUS AS OUR LORD

Our salvation occurs in a matter of seconds. The next stage of our relationship with God lasts the remainder of our lifetime: We obey and serve Jesus as our Lord. From that morning when

I was twelve to this morning, I am a follower of Jesus Christ. He is the Master. He is the Author and Finisher of my faith. He is the Teacher. He is the Source of all power, blessing, and direction in my life.

Prior to our salvation, we serve the devil—consciously or unconsciously, willfully or carelessly. After our salvation, we are called to serve the Lord Jesus Christ. We are challenged to walk in His footsteps and to bring glory to His name. Our life's purpose is to be a witness to His love and mercy, and to be conformed into His likeness of character.

The primary way we serve the Lord is by doing what He has commanded us to do. Jesus said to His disciples:

> He who has My commandments and keeps them, it is he who loves Me. (John 14:21)

> If anyone loves Me, he will keep My word; and My Father will love him, and We will come to him and make Our home with him. (John 14:23)

> Abide in My love. If you keep My commandments, you will abide in My love, just as I have kept My Father's commandments and abide in His love. (John 15:9–10)

Serving Jesus as Lord is all about obedience, submission of our will to His, being sensitive to His daily guidance, and being committed to fulfilling His will for our lives.

We should note at this point that not everybody who hears

the gospel message accepts Jesus as Savior. All are invited to accept Him, but relatively few do. Furthermore, not everybody who accepts Jesus as Savior will follow through and remain committed to following Jesus as Lord. Relatively few will choose to keep His commandments and serve Him with their whole hearts. All are commanded and authorized and invited to experience the rewards that come from being a genuine disciple and servant of the Lord. But not all obey or choose to heed His voice and do His will.

There's a third phase that is made available to all who serve Jesus as Lord. Just as with receiving Jesus and following Him as a disciple, not all believers choose to enter this phase of their relationship with God. It is wise to do so, but not all choose.

THE THIRD PHASE OF OUR RELATIONSHIP WITH GOD: WE LOVE JESUS AS OUR FRIEND

All who call Jesus Savior and Lord are invited to be His friend.

What kind of friend is Jesus? He is the *best* friend you will ever have. He does for us what no one else can do, He helps us in ways no one else can help us, and He loves us as no one else can ever love us.

We may have difficulty seeing Jesus as our Friend, but Jesus doesn't have any difficulty seeing us that way. Consider the people Jesus called friend.

- *A stranger in need.* In the gospel of Luke we read a story about a paralyzed man who was brought to Jesus by four of his friends. These friends tore a hole in the roof of the house where Jesus was teaching, and they lowered their friend into His presence. Jesus said to this man, "Friend, your sins are forgiven you" (Luke 5:20 NASB).

This man didn't know very much about Jesus. He wasn't able to do anything for Jesus; he may not even have been able to talk to Him. Yet Jesus took the initiative and called this man "friend."

- *Sinners seeking a savior.* Also in the gospel of Luke we find an incident in which Jesus was criticized for associating with people whom the religious leaders deemed to be sinners. Jesus responded to their criticism by saying, "For John the Baptist came neither eating bread nor drinking wine, and you say, 'He has a demon.' The Son of Man has come eating and drinking, and you say, 'Look, a glutton and a winebibber, a friend of tax collectors and sinners!'" (Luke 7:33–34).

  Jesus was not afraid to associate with those who were outcasts of society. He did not seek perfect people as His friends—rather He made friends out of imperfect people. He touched their lives, and in their response to Him, a bond was formed. John later wrote of Jesus, "We love Him because He first loved us" (1 John 4:19).

- *Followers in the crowd.* In Luke 12, Jesus took on the hypocrisy of the Pharisees. He said to the people who were following Him, "And I say to you, My friends, do not be afraid of those who kill the body, and after that have no more that they can do. But I will show you whom you should fear: Fear Him who, after He has killed, has power to cast into hell; yes, I say to you, fear Him!" (Luke 12:4–5).

Jesus regarded all those who followed Him as His friends—that surely includes us today.

- *A close associate.* In John, we find the story of Jesus raising Lazarus from the dead. The story begins with Jesus receiving word that Lazarus is sick. He delays going to Lazarus for two more days, however, and then He says to His disciples: "Our friend Lazarus sleeps, but I go that I may wake him up" (John 11:11).

  Jesus was a visitor in the home of Lazarus, the brother of Mary and Martha of Bethany, on numerous occasions. Jesus considered Lazarus to be His friend, even though he was not one of the twelve disciples or a close follower of His ministry in Galilee, where Jesus spent most of His time.

- *A disciple who betrayed Him.* In the Garden of Gethsemane, Judas approached Jesus to betray Him, and Jesus said as Judas kissed Him, "Friend, why have you come?" (Matt. 26:50). Yes, Jesus even called the man who betrayed Him "friend."

  Now if Jesus calls casual acquaintances—sick or well, notorious sinners, general followers in the crowd—and even a disloyal disciple "friends," surely you qualify to be a friend of Jesus! Jesus sees each one of us as a potential friend—He desires to be our Friend even if we do not accept His friendship.

Jesus extends friendship to all who follow Him. On the night before He was betrayed and crucified, Jesus met with His close disciples in an upper room. He said to them:

> This is My commandment, that you love one another as I have loved you. Greater love has no one than this, than to lay down one's life for his friends. You are My friends if you do whatever I command you. No longer do I call you servants, for a servant does not know what his master is doing; but I have called you friends, for all things that I heard from My Father I have made known to you. You did not choose Me, but I chose you and appointed you that you should go and bear fruit, and that your fruit should remain, that whatever you ask the Father in My name He may give you. These things I command you, that you love one another. (John 15:12–17)

If you are a follower of Jesus today, He calls you to be His friend.

YOUR LEVEL OF ACCEPTANCE DETERMINES YOUR LEVEL OF RELATIONSHIP

If you have never intentionally, actively received Jesus as your Savior . . . why not do so today? If you have never intentionally, actively received Jesus' imparting of the Holy Spirit to you . . . why not do so today? If you have never intentionally, actively received Jesus as your Friend . . . why not do so today?

The degree to which you intentionally and actively accept the relationship that God offers to you is the degree to which the Lord will reveal Himself to you and impart His wisdom to you.

THE DISTINCTIVE HALLMARKS OF FRIENDSHIP WITH JESUS

Let me point out to you four distinct ways in which Jesus truly is the Friend of friends in our lives.

1. SACRIFICIAL LOVE

The foremost hallmark of Jesus' friendship with us is His sacrificial love. Numerous stories have been told through the ages of people who sacrificed their own lives to save others. Soldiers have thrown themselves on land mines or taken bullets to save their comrades. Casual passersby have thrown themselves into raging fires and swirling waters, have hurled themselves into the paths of runaway cars and trains, and have entered other highly dangerous situations to save total strangers. Most of these acts of courage and self-sacrifice are instantaneous responses. Many brave people who have survived their own acts of bravery have said, "I didn't think—I just responded in the moment. I did what I instinctively knew was the right thing to do."

Jesus knew what He was doing when He went to the cross. His sacrifice was purposeful, intentional, and deliberate. He knew that God's plan was for Him to sacrificially lay down His life so we might be given the opportunity to receive God's forgiveness, be freed from the power of sin over our lives, and live with Him forever.

The apostle Paul wrote,

> For when we were still without strength, in due time Christ died for the ungodly. For scarcely for a righteous man will one die; yet perhaps for a good man someone would even dare to die. But God demonstrates His own love toward us, in that while we were still sinners, Christ died for us . . . For if when we were enemies we were reconciled to God through the death of His Son, much more, having been reconciled, we shall be saved by His life. (Rom. 5:6–8, 10)

Jesus chose to die for us out of His infinite, unconditional love for us. His life was not taken from Him—He purposefully and willfully laid it down in order that you and I might become His eternal friends (John 10:18).

Nobody else can love you as much as Jesus loved you in dying for you. A person may die on your behalf to save your life . . . but nobody else can ever die to save your eternal soul. No sacrifice that any other person makes can ever equal what Jesus has done on your behalf.

2. AN ONGOING INITIATIVE

Jesus takes the initiative in establishing a friendship with you. He said to His disciples: "You did not choose Me, but I chose you" (John 15:16).

Jesus did not take the initiative on the basis of our worthiness, works, or character. He chose us while we were sinners. He chose us so He might save us, heal us, restore us to a right relationship with the Father, and walk with us in intimate friendship the rest of our lives. He chose us to carry out and fulfill His plan and purpose.

Why is it important for us to recognize this quality in our friendship with Jesus Christ? Because if we have any idea at all that we are the ones who are initiating a relationship with God—Father, Son, and Holy Spirit—we are going to strive to win God's approval and acceptance. We are going to try to earn His friendship on the basis of our own efforts, good deeds, or self-denial.

When we face the truth that Jesus initiated a relationship with us, we must lay down our pride—our friendship with God is the result of nothing that we have done or can ever do. We must be willing to lay down our pride and humbly receive what He has done on our behalf. We must accept His death on the cross as being on our behalf. We must receive His indwelling presence in the form of the Holy Spirit. We must gratefully acknowledge that He is the One who paid the price in full for our friendship with God. As Paul wrote so eloquently to the Ephesians, "For by grace you have been saved through faith, and that not of yourselves; it is the gift of God, not of works, lest anyone should boast" (Eph. 2:8–9).

You may be the one who generally takes the initiative in establishing a friendship with another person—or you may be the reluctant one who waits and hopes that someone you would like to have as a friend will seek you out. Either way, no human being does what Jesus does in taking the initiative of friendship. Human friendships are built on give-and-take, on a certain degree of compromise, and on both parties being willing to express care and concern for the other. Jesus' friendship with us is built on a basis of His giving and our receiving. There is no compromise—He loves us in a way that is unconditional, absolute, and infinite. Either we receive Him or we don't; there are no halfway markers. No person is ever "almost saved" or "nearly saved."A person has accepted Jesus as Savior, or he hasn't.

Furthermore, Jesus extends His love and concern to us in spite of our failure to respond. He gives and gives and gives. No matter how much we serve God, praise God, love God, engage in ministry efforts for God, we will never come close to repaying Him for all He has done for us. We will never be on an equal footing with Jesus when it comes to initiating acts of love, mercy, forgiveness, and grace.

Accept that truth. Praise God for always taking the initiative toward you. Praise God that His mercies to you are new every morning—He is continually extending Himself to you and seeking ways in which to bless you, guide you, and encourage you (Lam. 3:22–23).

3. REVOLUTIONARY AND POSITIVE CHANGE IN US

When we become a friend of Jesus, something revolutionary happens inside us. Our spirits, our hearts, our souls, our destinies, our perspectives on life, and our capacities to love all change dramatically. We become a "new creation," and our minds begin to be renewed so that we see things as Jesus saw them, feel things as Jesus felt them, and respond to life as Jesus responded (2 Cor. 5:17 and Eph. 4:20–24). We begin to understand the "good and acceptable and perfect will of God" (Rom. 12:2).

Jesus gives to us something far more valuable than any human friend can ever give: He reveals to us the truth about God . . . the truth about ourselves . . . the truth about the relationship He desires to have with us . . . and the truth He desires for us to have with other human beings. He reveals in His own presence within us the whole truth, and nothing but the truth. He is Truth.

Jesus reveals to us things that we can never know any other way, and He enables us to do things we could never do by any other source of power. Jesus teaches us not only God's commandments and how to apply them on this earth, but He empowers us to keep and to do God's commandments. He said to His disciples: "I . . . appointed you that you should go and bear fruit, and that your fruit should remain, that whatever you ask the Father in My name He may give you" (John 15:16).

On what basis do we bear eternal fruit? On the basis of keeping His commandments and by loving one another as we abide in His love.

Those are the two important stipulations Jesus gave to His disciples in His last meeting with them before His crucifixion. He said to them:

> If you keep My commandments, you will abide in My love, just as I have kept My Father's commandments and abide in His love. (John 15:10)

This is My commandment, that you love one another
as I have loved you . . . These things I command you, that
you love one another. (John 15:12, 17)

Jesus told His disciples, both in His words and by His life, about what it means to trust God in all things. He revealed to them the big picture of life—telling them about heaven and hell and the consequences of accepting Him as their Savior. He taught them how to pray, how to respond to persecution, how to deal with evil, how to exercise faith in bringing healing and deliverance to those in need. He revealed to them the immediate future and the tasks He desired for them to do—He told them about the Resurrection, the Ascension, and their ministry on this earth after He returned to His heavenly home.

Everything that is required for a righteous, pure, wise life . . . Jesus taught His disciples through His sermons and through the example of His own life. And through His Word today, Jesus teaches us all that we need to accept Him, follow Him, and live with Him forever.

When we have a friendship with Jesus, our lives take on a completely new quality and nature. We are indwelled by His Holy Spirit. Our lives automatically move away from sin and toward purity. Our lives begin to reflect the character of the Holy Spirit: love, joy, peace, patience, kindness, goodness, faithfulness, gentleness, and self-control (Gal. 5:22–23).

A friend may influence your life, but no human friend can ever totally transform your life from the inside out in the way Jesus Christ does.

And when we respond to Jesus with our love and devotion, the more He expands our ability to love others and to minister to them. The more we receive His love, the more love we have to pour out.

The change Jesus brings into our lives includes a tremendous challenge to become more than we presently are. Jesus is not a friend who leaves us in our weakness, winks at our sin, or allows us to continue in error. No! He accepts us where we are, but at the same time, He challenges us to move toward wholeness, perfection, and genuine excellence. He challenges us to become all that our Creator designed us to be and to do. He equips us with His presence so we can move from where we are to where He desires for us to be.

Jesus challenged His disciples:

> He who believes in Me, the works that I do he will do also; and greater works than these he will do, because I go to My Father. And whatever you ask in My name, that I will do, that the Father may be glorified in the Son. If you ask anything in My name, I will do it. (John 14:12–14)

Jesus challenged His disciples to learn all that the Holy Spirit would teach them. He challenged them to allow the Holy Spirit to guide them into all truth and to empower them to be witnesses of Him. Jesus challenged His disciples to be per-fect—to be made whole and complete—to lay down their old lives and pick up the new life He would give them.

The apostle Paul reiterated Jesus' challenge when he encouraged the early believers to "put off" the old man and all its "deceitful lusts." He called them to "put on the new man which was created according to God, in true righteousness and holiness" (Eph. 4:24).

No friend will ever challenge you to the heights that Jesus challenges you. And even if you have a very encouraging friend who seeks to build you up continually, that friend can never actually help you do or become all that Jesus promises to help you accomplish and to be.

Whatever Jesus commands us to do, He enables us to do. He is a Friend who not only tells us what to do, but a Friend who walks through life with us every step of the way, guiding us and empowering us to live out the life He Himself led.

4. ABIDING PRESENCE

Jesus never leaves us or forsakes us (Heb. 13:5). He is with us always. In His own words, Jesus said, "Lo, I am with you always, even to the end of the age" (Matt. 28:20).

No matter how much time a friend may spend with you, no friend can be with you twenty-four hours a day, seven days a week, every day of the year, every year for the rest of your life.

When you are in the valley in despair . . . He's there.

When you arrive at the top of the mountain in triumph . . . He's there.

The old adage is true: When things get thick, friends tend to thin out. That is never true of Jesus, however. He stands by us always. No persecution is ever too intense or criticism too severe for Him to turn away from you. He is there not only up to the point of your death, but He is with you through your death and is with you on the other side of death. No other friend can ever make that claim.

OUR FRIEND OF FRIENDS

Who is your very best friend? No matter who that friend may be, there's an even *better* Friend. This Friend will never misunderstand you . . . never disappoint you . . . and never abandon you or reject you.

Jesus loves you unconditionally. His love for you is infinite and merciful. Jesus accepts you just the way you are. He never expects you to "get good" before you "get God"—to the contrary, He desires for you to receive Him so He can help you in every area of your life.

Jesus has time for you. He is never too busy for you. He will listen to you, no matter what you desire to say to Him. Jesus has answers for you. No matter what problem or difficulty you are facing, Jesus has a way out of your negative situation. He will speak to you through His Word and through the Holy Spirit prompting you to take godly actions. Jesus not only gives us answers about life, but He readily reveals to us Himself. He is quick to show us how He works, what He desires, how much He loves, and the depth of His concern. He will answer any question you ever have about who He is.

Jesus forgives you. He never holds a grudge or puts up a barrier to forgiving all your sins. He completely erases your sinful past—He alone has the full capacity to forgive and forget.

Jesus understands you and cares for you. There isn't any situation in your life that is beyond His awareness, His concern, and His tender care. Jesus understands your hurts and cries with you. He shares your pain and sorrow. He never abandons you in a time of trial or suffering.

Jesus never condemns you for your failures. To the contrary, when you fail, He picks you up, dusts you off, and helps you to move forward in your life. He teaches you important lessons from your mistakes so you can experience strength and wholeness.

Jesus never stops giving to you. He continually is seeking ways to bless you and to build you up from the inside out. His desire always is that you might be blessed and prosper in your spirit, mind, body, relationships, finances, and in all other ways (3 John 2). Jesus always desires the best for us—in every circumstance, every job, and every relationship.

Jesus never stops touching you. He continually causes others who believe in Him to come to you to give you the hug, the words of comfort, and the close presence you need. He lives in and through His followers today, compelling people to speak to you, do for you, and touch you in His name so that you receive the help you need.

There are also those times when Jesus makes His presence to us so real that it seems as if He is right there with us. His presence is palpable. We have no doubt that He is with us. I have only experienced that three times in my life but each time was so vivid that I can recall exactly where I was, what I was doing, and how the presence of Jesus felt.

Jesus confronts us when we neglect Him, disobey Him, or move in ways that will bring us or others harm. He loves us enough to correct us.

Jesus is utterly faithful. Whatever He says He will do, He does. You can count on His promises. His commitment to you is lasting. All that Jesus is, He will always be. His friendship never changes.

Jesus will be with us for all eternity. He has built us a heavenly home and will live with us forever.

Oh, what a Friend we have in Jesus!

A sacrificial love.

An ongoing initiative toward us.

A revolutionary positive change in us and an empowering challenge for us to excel and become whole.

An abiding presence.

No other friend can ever do for us what Jesus has done, is doing, and will do . . . not only today but also forever.

The questions we must ask ourselves today are these:

Am I wisely pursuing a friendship with Jesus?

What kind of a friend am I to Him?

KEEP WALKING!

I t's one thing to start out on a path God calls you to follow . . . it's another thing to continue to walk out that path day in and day out, year in and year out, perhaps for decades or a lifetime. It's one thing to accept Jesus Christ and to experience the exuberance of knowing that your sins are forgiven, you have been filled with God's Holy Spirit, and you are called into a newness of life. It's another thing to walk out the Christian life in wisdom month after month, problem after problem, difficulty after difficulty.

How long are you to persevere in the thing to which God calls you? Until God leads you into something else. You are to remain where you are, doing what God has called you to do, until the moment when God initiates a change.

Many voices will call to you to lure you away from God's wise path. You must say "no" to those voices, even when the allure is powerful, the temptation is strong, the rewards seem bright, or the detour seems easy.

How can you determine if you should continue walking on the path God has set you on? Look over your shoulder at your own footprints. Are your footprints in keeping with Scripture? Have you walked wisely? Look at the path ahead. Is the path ahead one that leads to righteousness and God's reward—is it the path that God has led you to walk? If so . . . stay on the path!

Get God's viewpoint.

Do what the Word of God tells you to do.

Follow the promptings of the Holy Spirit.

And you will know how to walk wisely.

Determine in your heart that you will choose God's way over your own way.

Determine in your heart that you will trust God day by day.

Persevere in what God directs you to do.

And you will walk in wisdom . . . all the way to eternity's door.

ABOUT THE AUTHOR

CHARLES STANLEY is pastor of the 14,000-member First Baptist Church in Atlanta, Georgia. He is the speaker on the internationally popular radio and television program *In Touch*.

Twice elected president of the Southern Baptist Convention, Stanley received his bachelor of arts degree from the University of Richmond, his bachelor of divinity degree from Southwestern Theological Seminary, and his master's and doctor's degrees from Luther Rice Seminary.

Don't Miss These Books
by Charles Stanley

———•———

from Thomas Nelson Publishers

A Gift of Love

Beloved pastor and Bible teacher Charles Stanley invites us to experience, accept, and share God's intense love for us. He wants us to accept God's gift of love—His Son. Ultimately, he encourages us to share God's extraordinary love with those around us.

Charles Stanley's Handbook for Christian Living

Tired of searching through impersonal, complicated commentaries for answers to life's tough questions? With unique graphics, inviting page designs, and rich commentary from beloved pastor Charles Stanley, *Charles Stanley's Handbook for Christian Living* is a refreshing alternative to typical Bible commentaries.

On Holy Ground

Abraham leaving Ur for an unknown land God would show him. Jesus going out into the wilderness of temptation. Paul's life-changing trip down the Damascus road. All of these biblical journeys offer insight into our own personal spiritual journey. In *On Holy Ground*, Charles Stanley takes an in-depth look at twelve such biblical journeys to show us how we, too, can meet God and follow where He leads.

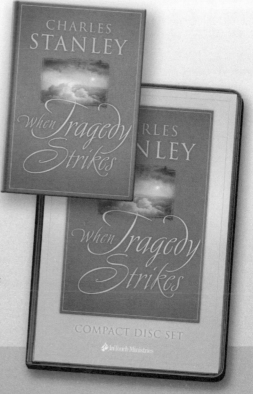

OTHER RESOURCES FROM CHARLES STANLEY

Walking Wisely
Audio or video kit

Have you ever gone hiking and lost your way? One or two wrong turns can leave you disoriented or even totally lost. Dr. Stanley teaches that as you walk with God, His Word will serve as the compass that guides your steps and assures your safety.

Two-tape audio set with workbook
Order WWSET $29.95 (Canada $40.95)

Two-tape video set with workbook
Order VWWSET 29.95 (Canada $40.95)

Workbook
Order WWKB $8.95 (Canada 11.95)

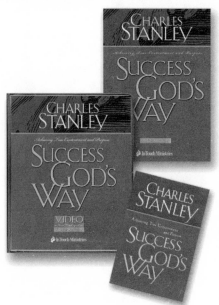

Success God's Way
Audio, video, compact disc kit,
or hardcover book

What is the secret to your success? Is it talent, education, or maybe leadership? These qualities are fine, but true success starts and ends with God's Word. Dr. Stanley teaches that only as we read, study, apply, and obey the Scriptures can we enjoy true and lasting success.

The Success God's Way kit includes 10 hours of teaching on 10 audio or 4 videotapes, plus a 200-page workbook. You may also order it in a 10 compact-disc kit, workbook included!

Ten-CD set with workbook / Order SGWSETCD $74.95 (Canada $99.95)

Ten-tape audio set with workbook / Order SGWSET $74.95 (Canada $99.95)

Four-tape video set with workbook / Order VSGWSET $74.95 (Canada $99.95)

Hardcover book, 256 pages / Order SGWBK $20 (Canada $27)

IN TOUCH MINISTRIES® P.O. Box 7900 Atlanta, Georgia 30357
IN TOUCH MINISTRIES OF CANADA Box 4900 Markham, Ontario L3R 6G9
800-323-3747 (US and Canada)
www.intouch.org